A Walk in and around Ronda

This walk starts in the Plaza de España and takes you across the bridge to explore the old town of Ronda.

From the Plaza de España walk towards the Puente Nuevo (New Bridge, ➤ 44).

Take a walk around the Parador, on the right, for spectacular views of the gorge. Return and cross over the bridge, taking a look down into the ravine as you pass.

A right turn into Calle Tenorio will take you into a network of narrow streets and neat white houses leading to the Plaza del Campillo. Keep walking and at the far end look for steps leading down the hill.

A short walk down reveals Ronda's houses perched on the clifftop. Going on further will provide you with a classic view of the bridge, but it's a long climb back up!

Back up again take the small street ahead to the Plaza Mondragón.

On the right is the Palacio de Mondragón, once a Moorish palace.

Continue to Plaza de la Duquesa de Parcént. A left turn leads to the entrance of the Colegiata de Santa María la Mayor. Take the short slope down to Calle Armiñán and turn left. Note the Minaret of San Sebastián before crossing over to turn sharp right.

There are fine carvings on the façade of the Palacio del Marqués de Salvatierra (closed to the public).

Climb up Calle Santo Domingo to the Casa del Rey Moro, where you can take a long winding staircase down to the river and back up again to the gardens. Rejoin Calle Armiñán and cross back over the bridge to end your walk in the Plaza de España.

INFORMATION

Distance 4km
Time 2–3 hours
Start/end point Plaza de España
Lunch Pedro Romero (€€)
✉ Virgen de la Paz 18, Ronda
☎ 952 87 11 10

Ronda's whitewashed houses add to the town's charm

A Drive to Antequera

INFORMATION

Distance 125km
Time About 6 hours
Start/end point Torremolinos
✚ D2
Lunch Parador de Antequera (€€)
✉ García del Olmo, Antequera
☎ 952 84 02 61

This drive offers some striking scenery, taking you first to Antequera and continuing to the strange twisted rock formations in the El Torcal Natural Park.

From Torremolinos turn onto the N340 towards Málaga. Passing the airport on your left, continue on the Málaga ring road (Ronda de Málaga) and follow the signs to Antequera (N331).

After the turn-off to Finca de la Concepción the highway climbs up through the hills of the Montes de Málaga, scattered with olive groves and tiny white houses. As you approach Antequera dramatic rock shapes rise from the fertile plains, noticeably the striking form of the so-called Peña de los Enamorados (Lovers' Rock). About an hour after departure you should enter Antequera (► 25). Allow time to explore this attractive city of churches and convents.

Attractive Antequera

Take the Calle de la Legión in a southerly direction. A few moments out of town pause to admire the magnificent views of Antequera on your left, backed by the distinctive form of the Peña de los Enamorados. Take the C3310, following the signs to Torcal.

The road winds through a barren landscape of rocks and boulders for about half an hour before reaching a right turn to Parque Natural El Torcal (► 41). As you drive through the park, the rocks and boulders become increasingly bizarre, until the whole landscape appears positively lunar-like. The road ends some 15 minutes later by a small hut. Walking trails start from here.

Rejoin the C3310 and continue south to the coast and return to Torremolinos.

A Walk around Antequera

This walk takes in some of Antequera's many churches and includes magnificent views. Most churches close from 1.30pm to 4pm so a morning walk is recommended.

INFORMATION

Distance 4.5km
Time About 3 hours
Start point Plaza San Sebastián
End point Plaza del Portichuelo
Lunch Restaurante El Angelote (€€)
✉ Plaza Caso Viejo
☎ 952 70 34 65

On the Plaza San Sebastián look at the 16th-century Colegiata de San Sebastián. Walk up Calle Infante Don Fernando. Take a look at the Iglesia de San Agustín, on the left, and further along, on the right, you will pass the Palacio Consistorial (Town Hall) and the Convento de los Remedios.

Just past the Iglesia de San Juan de Dios turn sharp right into Calle Cantareros and back towards the centre.

You will pass the house of the Condado de Colchado and the Convento de la Madre de Dios de Monteagudo.

A steep street in Antequera, with the Nerja Palace standing above

Continue down Calle Diego Ponce, then turn left up to Plaza San Francisco and the Plazuela de San Zoilo. This brings you to the Convento Real de San Zoilo, one of Antequera's National Monuments, and some fine views.

Take Calle Calzada and continue up Cuesta de Los Rojos to Plaza del Carmen. On Calle del Carmen is the Iglesia del Carmen. Return and take a sharp right, turn up Calle del Colegio, a very steep climb, to the Arco de los Gigantes (Arch of Giants) on your left.

Pass through the arch to the Real Colegiata de Santa María la Mayor. Nearby are the Roman Baths.

Return through the Arch and go left along Calle Herradores to the charming Plaza del Portichuelo on which stands the Iglesia de Santa María de Jesús.

A Walk through Málaga's Old Town

This walk starts in the Plaza de la Marina. It's a thorough tour of Málaga's old quarters, and takes in the cathedral and several churches.

INFORMATION

Distance 4km
Time 2–3 hours, depending on visits to churches
Start/end point Plaza de la Marina
Lunch La Posada de Antonio (€€)
✉ Calle Granada 33
☎ 952 17 26 29

Top: *Plaza de la Merced*
Above: *the narrow streets of Málaga's Old Town*

From Plaza de la Marina take Calle Molina Lario, left of the Málaga Palacio Hotel facing you. A few moments' walk will bring you right up to the cathedral.

Horses and carriages line up here ready to take visitors on a tour around the town. Opposite, on the Plaza Obispo, is the old Palacio Episcopal, which contains delightful 'hidden' patios and has exhibitions of contemporary art.

Turn right along Calle Santa María and continue along Calle San Agustín.

On your right is the Palacio Buenavista, which now houses the Museo Picasso (► 54).

Take a right fork into Calle Granada, which takes you by the Iglesia de Santiago. Almost opposite is tiny Calle Tomás de Cózar 13 leading to Malaga's new El Hammam Arab Baths. After a brief pampering visit, continue along Calle Granada until you reach the Plaza de la Merced.

The centre of the Plaza de la Merced is marked by an obelisk in memory of General Torrijos and his men who were shot after the War of Independence. On the far corner, in an attractive block of houses, is the Casa Natal de Picasso, birthplace of Pablo Picasso, now centre of the Picasso Foundation (► 54).

Return down Calle Granada to Plaza del Siglo and on to the Plaza de la Constitucíon, then stroll down Calle Marqués Larios, Málaga's main shopping street. On the left take a short detour through the archway and along Pasaje de Chinitas, which leads to a tiny square – home to the tourist office. Complete the walk down Calle Marqués Larios and turn into the Alameda Principal to Plaza de la Marina.

A Coastal Drive to Gibraltar

This drive takes you along the coast through the Sotogrande development to the tiny British colony of Gibraltar.

From Estepona take the N340 coastal road south-west in the direction of Algeciras. The road follows the coast fairly closely for a while, passing through a string of *urbanizaciones* (developments). Some 10 minutes on you may wish to turn off and take a look at Duquesa Marina (follow the signs), another of the Costa's yacht-filled harbours. Continue on the N340.

You will soon enter the province of Cádiz and the community of Manilva. The road then passes through Sotogrande (known for golf and polo). Shortly after there is a turning to Puerto Sotogrande, a luxurious marina. Continue on the N340. This last section of the coastal road has been widened to dual carriageway. Ticket offices advertising ferry trips to Tangier and Centa signal the approach to the ferry ports.

Soon after, look for the turn-off to La Línea and follow the signs to La Línea–Gibraltar, 7km. Drive to La Línea and continue to the border with Gibraltar.

You are strongly advised to leave your car in the car park in La Línea, as you could face lengthy delays at the border when re-entering Spain, depending on the current political situation. There are also parking problems in Gibraltar itself. The car park at La Línea has ticket machines, with free parking on Sundays. Cross into Gibraltar on foot (you will need to show your passport). Guides are lined up here, ready to take you on a 60- to 90-minute tour, which includes a drive through town and up to St Michael's Cave where you can see dramatic rock formations. The drive continues steeply up through hairpin bends to see the famous apes and the sweeping views of the Mediterranean, Atlantic and south to Africa.

Return to La Línea to pick up your car, then take the N340 back to Estepona.

INFORMATION

Distance 105km
Time About 6 hours, allowing time to visit Gibraltar
Start/end point Estepona
B2
Lunch Da Paolo (€€)
Marina Bay, Gibraltar
9567 76 799
Remember to bring your passport

Top: *the Rock of Gibraltar*
Above: *spectacular lighting in St Michael's Cave*

Finding Peace & Quiet

If you want to take a break from the hustle and bustle of the Costa del Sol, there are many options to choose. The hinterland offers various landscapes, from olive groves in rolling hills to dramatic mountain ranges with snowcapped peaks. In a short time you can leave behind the heat of the coast and lose yourself in the tranquil surroundings of inland Andalucía.

GREEN TOURISM

The concept of green tourism is being developed by the regional government of Andalucía. The idea is to create an awareness of the countryside, allowing a chance to observe animals and plants in their natural habitat, enjoy home cooking and have contact with locals. A selection of accommodation offers this type of holiday and information can be obtained from: RAAR (Red Andaluza de Alojamientos Rurales), Apartado 2035, 04080 Almería ☎ 902 44 22 33, www.raar.es. Others offering rural holidays include the Asociación de Hoteles Rurales de Andalucía, Calle Ramal Hoyo, Torremolinos ☎ 952 37 87 75, www.ahra.es; Rustic Blue, Barrio La Ermita, Bubión, Granada ☎ 952 76 33 81, www.rusticblue.com; Casa Andaluza ☎ 956 45 60 53, www.casa-andaluza.com

NATURE PARKS AND RESERVES

A number of protected areas and nature parks lie within reach of the coast. Their landscapes of wild natural beauty and wealth of flora and fauna make them an ideal destination for the nature-lover seeking peace and quiet.

Among these are the Parque Natural Montes de Málaga, north of Málaga; and south of Antequera, the Parque Natural El Torcal, with its weird and wonderful rock formations (► 41). West from Marbella, you can easily reach the National Game Reserve near Monda, or the Parque Natural Sierra de Las Nieves, south of Ronda, with its rugged cliffs and great ravines.

Farther west still are the nature parks of Grazalema and Los Alcornocales, both areas of natural, unspoilt landscape. Southeast of Granada and easily accessible from the eastern section of the Costa del Sol is the Parque Natural Sierra Nevada, famed for its striking scenery and diversity of plant and animal life.

Horseriding on the beach gives beautiful views across the sea

HIKING AND HORSERIDING

The nature parks are wonderful areas for hikers and usually have marked trails for visitors to follow. Information on walking trails can be obtained from local tourist offices. The region of Las Alpujarras, with its varied scenery, also provides excellent walking terrain.

With its long tradition of raising and riding horses, Andalucía provides an ideal backdrop for long distance trekking. Stables are plentiful and horses can be hired to explore the coast and its hinterland.

RURAL ACCOMMODATION

Mountain refuges and Andalucían-style country houses make it possible to stay in some of these remote areas. They are often located in wild, mountainous terrain (although usually near access roads) and offer magnificent views.

BIRDWATCHING

Spring and autumn are good periods to watch the European bird migration. Using Spain's southern coast as a resting place, hundreds of species of birds stop here on their journey between Africa and northern Europe. Early morning is a good time to see new arrivals and vantage points are Punta Marroqui at Tarifa, Calahonda, east of Marbella, and Benalmádena.

The nature reserve at the mouth of the river Guadalhorce, just east of Torremolinos, is another good place for birdwatching. An area of exceptional beauty is the Laguna de Fuente de Piedra. Off the N343, west of Antequera, it is known as the Pink Lagoon, after the large colony of pink flamingos which comes here every year to breed. The best time to see these spectacular birds is from the end of January to June. The chicks hatch around April and May.

Inset: *a white hibiscus*
Below: *walking in the hills*

LAS ALPUJARRAS

The region of Las Alpujarras lies between the coastal sierras of Lujar, La Contraviesa and Gador and the Sierra Nevada. Its remoteness and inaccessibility has provided a haven to many a fugitive – from the Moors who fled here after the fall of Granada, to Republicans who sought refuge here after the civil war. It now has a growing appeal to expatriates seeking a more peaceful retreat.

What's On

JANUARY *Los Reyes Magos* (6 January). In Málaga and all the major coastal resorts, the Three Kings throw sweets to children from grand floats.

FEBRUARY/MARCH *Carnaval* (the week before Lent). In Málaga, Granada and Antequera. Exuberant floats, colourful costumes, music and dancing.

MARCH/APRIL *Semana Santa* (Holy Week, moveable date). In Sevilla, Málaga and Granada. From Palm Sunday to Easter Day there are nightly processions of *cofradías* (brotherhoods) carrying images of the saints or the Virgin; wearing pointed hoods, each carries a lighted candle. The muffled drums are accompanied by the occasional *saeta* (lament).

APRIL *Feria de Sevilla* (Sevilla Fair). Originally a cattle fair, the Fair has evolved into a world famous event of colour, music and flamenco. The daily horseback parade is a special attraction. Every afternoon bullfights take place in the Maestranza ring with the most famous of Spain's matadors.

MAY *Las Cruces de Mayo* (early May). Crosses decorated with real and paper flowers are placed in the streets and squares. The fiesta is particularly attractive in Torrox and Coín.

MAY/JUNE *Corpus Christi* (moveable date). Processions along flower strewn streets. Especially colourful in Granada, with parades, music and dancing.

JULY *La Virgen del Carmen* (16 July). Most spectacular at Los Boliches, Fuengirola; also at Estepona, Marbella and Nerja. The patron saint of fishermen is paraded through the streets before being taken around the bay on a boat. There are fireworks, music and dancing on the beach.

SEPTEMBER *Pedro Romero Fiestas* (early September). Ronda celebrates the bullfighter with *corridas Goyescas* (Goya-style bullfights), with top matadors.

OCTOBER *Feria del Rosario*. Celebrated in Fuengirola during the first two weeks in October. *Casetas* (clubhouses) of various societies and brotherhoods set up between Fuengirola and Los Boliches offer shows, food and drink. Also horseriding events, flamenco and fireworks.

DECEMBER *Fiesta de Verdiales* (29 December). In La Venta de San Cayetano, in Puerto de la Torre, Málaga. Colourfully attired *pandas* (musical groups) compete with each other. A lively event with music, food and wine.

OSTA DEL SOL's top 25 sights

The sights are shown on the maps on the inside front cover and inside back cover, numbered 1–25 alphabetically

Top **25**

Almuñécar

INFORMATION

- F3
- 84km east of Málaga
- Variety of restaurants
- Local bus services
- Few
- Avenida Europa-Palacete La Najarra
  958 63 11 25

Archaeological Museum

- Cueva de los Siete Palacios
- Tue–Sat 11–2, 6–8

The picturesque town of Almuñécar lies amid orchards of tropical fruits. Its castle was built on the site of a Moorish fortress.

Almuñécar is typical of so many villages in southern Spain, with its cluster of whitewashed houses rising up the hillside, crowned by an old castle. It is in the province of Granada, on the coastline now designated the Costa Tropical.

The town's history goes back to the time of the Phoenicians, with subsequent occupations by the Romans and the Moors. The Castillo de San Miguel stands on top of a rock, dividing two bays. It was built during the reign of Carlos V, over the site of a former Moorish fortress, and features a great square tower known as La Mazmorra.

The town itself is a delightful jumble of narrow, cobblestoned streets, climbing steeply to the summit. Do not miss a visit to the Ornithological Park at the foot of the hill. Here you can see brilliantly coloured parrots and rare birds in a beautiful setting of subtropical plants and flowers. The seafront is lined with apartment blocks, bars and restaurants, buzzing with life day and night during the season.

Also worth a visit is the small archaeological museum in the Cueva de los Siete Palacios, thought to have been a Roman reservoir. The museum has a display of artefacts from the area.

A look-out post at nearby Punta de la Mona gives sweeping views of the harbour and the Mediterranean.

The seafront at Almuñécar

Antequera

Antequera has great charm behind its busy, unpretentious face. The discovery of prehistoric tombs has given the town added importance.

Antequera is known for its convents, churches and elegant mansions, all showing a variety of architectural influences. Thanks to the good motorway from Málaga it is easy to reach and can be visited in a day. (For the town walk ➤ 17 and for the drive from Torremolinos ➤ 16.)

The town is dominated by the old castle, which offers excellent views of the surrounding plains. Nearby, the 16th-century church of Santa María la Mayor features a fine Mudéjar ceiling. The splendid bell towers of the churches of San Sebastián and San Augustín combine the Mudéjar and baroque styles. The church of El Carmen, formerly a convent, has been designated a national monument. It is noted for its rich interior and impressive wooden altar.

A group of Neolithic-Bronze Age burial chambers lies on Antequera's northeastern outskirts. Of the three caves, the most important is the Dólmen de Menga. Its large cavern contains a series of stones and columns supporting the huge slabs that form the roof, believed to date back to 2500BC.

The Parque Natural El Torcal de Antequera, 13km south of Antequera, covers an extensive area of grey limestone rocks and boulders that have been weathered over time to form the most fantastic shapes (➤ 41).

INFORMATION

- D1
- 54km north of Málaga
- Good choice of restaurants (€–€€€)
- From Málaga
- From Málaga
- Few
- *Feria de Primavera* (31 May–1/2 Jun); *Noche Flamenca de Santa María* (end Jul); August Fair (early Aug)
- Plaza San Sebastián 7 ☎ 952 70 25 05; www.antequera.es

Dólmen de Menga

- 1km northeast of Antequera
- Wed–Sat 9–6; Tue, Sun 9–3.30
- Free
- From Antequera
- From Antequera
- None

The Dólmen de Menga dates from around 2500BC

Casares

INFORMATION

- B2
- 105km west of Málaga
- Several restaurants
- Local buses
- Few
- Gaucín (➤ 50)
- August Fair (early Aug)
- Calle Villa 29
  952 89 41 26

With its mass of whitewashed houses clambering up the hillside, Casares has a reputation for being the most photogenic town in Andalucía. The views of the town are always spectacular, wherever you approach from.

Casares is easily accessible from the coast: a turning around 16km west of Estepona leads up into the hills of the Sierra Bermeja. While the drive itself takes you through a scenic route of hills and wooded areas, nothing prepares you for the spectacular view of Casares, with its white houses spread over the hill. The Moorish castle crowning the hill is evidence of Muslim rule, ended by the Christians in the mid-15th century.

Much of the charm of Casares can be discovered by strolling through its white, terraced streets up to the castle. On the way, take a look at the 17th-century church of San Sebastián, which contains a statue of the Virgen del Rosario del Campo. The castle was built in the 13th century on Roman foundations. The nearby 16th-century Church of the Incarnation retains its original Madéjar tower.

Picturesque Casares

The views become more spectacular as you continue to the summit. Here you will be rewarded by a panorama over olive groves, orchards and forests, out to the blue of the Mediterranean Sea. Take a look too at the local cemetery, which is beautifully kept and adorned with flowers – not to be missed.

Córdoba

Córdoba, with its breathtaking Great Mosque, is one of Andalucía's richest jewels. It has an engaging intimacy not found in Granada or Sevilla, and in its hidden corners you'll feel the spirit of an older Spain.

Spring and autumn are good times to visit Córdoba, to avoid the heat of summer and the harsh weather of winter. The city, overlooked by the Sierra de Córdoba, has many attractions and is best explored on foot. Bear in mind that some of its narrow streets do not easily fit pedestrians and cars at the same time! The Mezquita, or Great Mosque (➤ 28), is a stunning survivor of Moorish Andalucía. The Judería (old Jewish Quarter) is a delightful area of narrow cobbled streets and white houses. Brilliantly coloured flowers adorn small squares, and beautiful ornate patios can be seen through doorways. The Alcazar, the Palace of the Christian Kings, dates from the 13th century. There is a museum with superb Roman mosaics and beautiful, cool gardens.

Córdoba has a spectacular past. Tools found on the banks of the River Guadalquivir suggest that palaeolithic man lived here. Later, Córdoba was conquered by the Carthaginians, the Romans and the Moors. In 929, under Moorish rule, the Caliphate of Córdoba was established. With the founding of a university, Córdoba became a renowned centre of art and culture. This period saw the construction of the Mezquita, along with other fine buildings.

In the 11th and 12th centuries, Córdoba went into decline. After the city fell to the Christians in 1236, the Catholic Monarchs presided here while planning the reconquest of Granada and it was here that Queen Isabella granted Columbus the commission for his voyage of discovery.

INFORMATION

- See fold-out map
- 187km north of Málaga
- Estación de Autobuses, Plaza de las Tres Culturas ☎ 957 40 40 40
- Estación de RENFE, Avenida de América ☎ 902 24 02 02
- Few
- Easter ceremonies; Fair (5–end May); International Festival of Music, Theatre and Dance (Aug); National Festival of Folklore (Sep); Córdoba Patios Competition (May)
- Calle Torrijos 10 ☎ 957 47 12 35 www.turiscordoba.es

Tourists admire artwork outside Córdoba's Alcazar

Córdoba's La Mezquita

INFORMATION

- ✉ Torrijos y Cardenal Herrero
- ☎ 957 47 05 12
- Mon–Sat 10–6.30, Sun 2–6.30
- Moderate
- Many restaurants nearby (€–€€€)
- RENFE station, Plaza de las Tres Culturas
- Few

Of all the Moorish buildings to survive in Andalucía, the Great Mosque of Córdoba is the most Islamic in its form – and the most haunting.

The Mezquita (Great Mosque) of Córdoba remains as a testimony to the immense power of Islam at its height of domination on the peninsula. It was built in four stages between the 8th and 10th centuries and is one of the world's largest mosques.

The mosque might have a rather forbidding outward appearance, but this conceals beauties within. The main entrance is through the Puerta del Perdón, which leads into the Patio de los Naranjos (Courtyard of the Oranges). Once inside you will be confronted by columns of onyx, marble and granite. They are topped with decorated capitals and crowned by the striking red and white arches so characteristic of Moorish architecture. The light effects within this dim interior are sensational. There is a sense of awe and mysticism, special to this particular mosque, which lures the visitor back time and time again.

To find a Christian cathedral within the very heart of the mosque comes as something of a surprise. It was built in the 1520s on the orders of Habsburg Emperor Carlos V, who later regretted his decision. However, it does manage to blend fairly well into its surroundings.

Rising above the Puerta del Perdón is the bell tower, which offers splendid views of the city.

The bell tower

Córdoba's Palacio de Viana

In a city renowned for its patios and gardens, this grand mansion has earned the nickname 'Museum of Patios' for its delightful courtyards.

The Viana Palace warrants a visit to see the beautiful garden and 12 charming patios. These are tastefully designed and adorned with fountains, greenery and an abundance of flowers. Clusters of roses and jasmine mingle with bougainvillaea and geraniums, surrounding you with delightful colour and fragrance.

The mansion, which dates back to the 14th century, is considered one of Córdoba's finest examples of stately architecture. For several hundred years it was the residence of the Marquises de Viana, during which time many extensions were added to the original building.

In the 1980s a bank bought the palace and opened it up to the public. One-hour conducted tours allow you to view the Viana family's former private rooms. The interior combines Renaissance style with Moorish influences. Note the spendid Mudéjar ceiling above the stairway to the first floor. Collections of ceramics, antiques, period furniture and weapons are on show, along with works by painters from Córdoba.

INFORMATION

- ✉ Rejas de Don Gome 2
- ☎ 957 49 67 41
- 🕐 Oct–May, Mon–Fri 10–1, 4–6. Sat 10–1; mid-Jun to Sep 9–2. Closed 1–15 Jun, Sun, public hols
- Inexpensive
- ♿ Few

Top: *the column courtyard*
Below: *the Viana Palace is known for its beautiful garden and patios*

Top **25**

7

Frigiliana

INFORMATION

- E2
- 56km east of Málaga
- Some restaurants (€€)
- Local
- Few
- Nerja (➤ 39)
- *Día de la Cruz* (3 May); *Feria de San Antonio* (13 Jun)
- Plaza del Ingenio s/n
  952 53 31 26

A short drive up into the hills from Nerja will take you to the pretty Andalusian village of Frigiliana, which has won several awards for its excellent state of conservation.

Frigiliana spreads its dazzling whitewashed houses out over the slopes of the Sierra Tejeda in two sections. The older part is a mass of narrow, cobbled streets winding their way up the hillside, with wonderful views over fertile orchards and the coast. Streets and balconies are decked out with colourful flowers and here and there you may come across a donkey patiently carrying its load. The village continues to attract a growing number of visitors. There are plenty of craft shops and galleries and several restaurants with outdoor terraces offering fine views.

One of the last battles between the Christians and the Moors was fought in the area in 1569, resulting in victory for the Christians. This event is narrated on a series of ceramic tiles on the walls of the houses.

You'll find plenty of opportunities to buy souvenirs in Frigiliana

Granada

Granada is one of Spain's crowning glories, the last kingdom of the Moors. The city is backed by the snowy peaks of the Sierra Nevada, a fitting setting for the renowned Alhambra Palace.

The priority for most visitors is La Alhambra (▶ 32). Magical as this Moorish palace is, it is surrounded by some equally fascinating places. The summer palace of El Generalife, with its shady avenues, water gardens, fountains and airy gazebos, is a neighbour of La Alhambra that you really should visit. On the slopes of the hill facing La Alhambra is the picturesque old Moorish quarter of Albaicín, a labyrinth of steep, narrow streets and small squares which has changed little with time. To the east rises the hill of Sacramonte, formerly the home of cave-dwelling gypsies.

Granada's other attractions range from the stately cathedral and the remarkable buildings of the university quarter to fashionable shopping streets and bazaar-like alleyways. For a real insight into the city's spirit, try to visit when a festival is taking place.

Known as Iliberis during the Iberian culture, Granada was taken by the Romans and the Visigoths before its conquest by the Moors in 711. The 11th century saw the beginning of the Kingdom of Granada. From the 13th century, until its downfall at the end of the 16th century, Granada flourished as a prosperous cultural centre with the construction of magnificent buildings such as La Alhambra. In 1492 Granada was taken by the Catholic Monarchs, marking the end of Moorish rule. The city continued to prosper during the Renaissance but a decline set in after a Moorish uprising was crushed in the 16th century.

INFORMATION

- F1
- 129km northeast of Málaga
- Estación de Autobuses, Carretera de Jaén s/n
  ☎ 958 18 54 80/98
- Estación de FFCC, Avenida de Andalucía s/n
  ☎ 958 20 40 00
- Few
- *Día de la Toma* (1, 2 Jan); *Semana Santa* (Easter); Corpus Christi; International Music and Dance Festival (end Jun, early Jul); *Romería* (29 Sep); International Jazz Festival (Nov)
- Corral del Carbón, Plaza de Mariana Pineda, 10 Bajo
  ☎ 958 24 71 28

An attractive fountain in the Plaza Nueva

Granada's La Alhambra

INFORMATION

- F1
- Calle Real s/n
- 958 02 79 00
- Mar–Oct daily 8.30–8. Night visits Tue–Sat, Sat 10pm–11.30pm. Access to Palacios Nazaries: 10–10.45 Nov–Feb daily. Night visits 8.30–6, Fri, Sat 8–9.30. Access to Palacios Nazaries 8–8.45
- Expensive (free for senior citizens, people with disabilities and Sun after 3pm) Snack kiosk
- Alhambrabus from city centre Few
- If you do not have a pre-booked ticket, arrive very early and be prepared to queue, as the number of tickets sold on site is restricted. Booking in advance is strongly recommended. Reservations can be made through the bank BBV 00 34 915 37 91 78 (abroad), 902 22 44 60 (within Spain), or online at www.alhambratickets.com

La Alhambra is the greatest surviving expression of Moorish culture in Spain, and is one of the world's most spectacular heritage sites.

The Alhambra holds a commanding position above the city of Granada, backed by the snowcapped peaks of the Sierra Nevada. In 1984 it joined UNESCO's list of World Heritage sites. Built by the Moors between the 13th and 15th centuries, it was used as a residence by Muhammad I and members of the Nasrid dynasty.

Walk up to the entrance from the Plaza Nueva. To the east is the Renaissance palace of Emperor Carlos V, started in 1526 but never completed. To the west stands the Alcazaba, the oldest building on the site. Climb up to the top of the Vela tower for breathtaking views of Granada and the Sierra Nevada.

A tour of the interior of the Casa Real (Royal Palace) reveals the true marvels of the Alhambra: the beautifully decorated Patio de Mexuar, the attractive Patio de los Arrayanes (named after the myrtle trees which line a rectangular pool) and the sumptuous Salón de los Embajadores (Ambassadors' Hall) with its richly carved and coffered ceiling. The Sala de los Abencerrajes has an impressive stalactite ceiling, and the Sala de las Dos Hermanas (Hall of the Two Sisters) features a delicate honeycomb dome. The focal point is the Patio de los Leones (Courtyard of Lions) named after the 12 stone lions which surround the central fountain (pictured left).

On the nearby Cerro del Sol (Hill of the Sun) stands the Palacio del Generalife. Dating back to the early 1300s, it was the summer palace of the Moorish kings. The gardens exude an aura of romance, with pools and fountains amid greenery, flowers and the resident cats.

Top **25**

10

Granada's Capilla Real

The Royal Chapel was built as a sepulchre for the Catholic Monarchs Ferdinand and Isabella, one of the most terrifying double acts in history.

Work began on the chapel in 1506 and was completed under the reign of the Habsburg Emperor Carlos V in 1521.

The chapel is an intriguing Gothic building, an odd mixture of the flamboyant and the constrained. It is impressive, if lacking the subtle elegance of Moorish buildings.

Inside lies the Renaissance monument of Carrara marble celebrating the two monarchs. Note how the head of Isabella's effigy is more deeply sunk into her pillow than Ferdinand's – a reflection, it is said, of her undoubtedly superior intelligence. Below the monument, down narrow steps, lie the lead coffins of the monarchs, their daughter Juana La Loca and her husband Philip the Fair, although there is no certainty that they contain the remains of anyone.

The most striking feature of the chapel is the altar's superb retablo (altarpiece), a gilded extravaganza.

A museum reached through the north arm of the transept displays items of historical interest and inclcudes a fine collection of paintings and sculpture.

INFORMATION

- F1
- Oficios 3 (Cathedral)
- 958 22 78 48
- 1 Apr–31 Oct Mon–Sat 10.30–1, 4–7, Sun 11–1, 4–7
- Inexpensive
- RENFE station Granada
- Few

Below: *The impressive exterior of the Capilla Real*

Málaga

INFORMATION

- D2
- Well served by buses from the coastal resorts
- Centro-Alameda railway station
- Many restaurants and tapas bars
- Pasaje de Chinitas 4 952 21 34 45; www.andalucia.org
- A good way to visit the city is by the electric train that runs half-hourly between Fuengirola and Málaga, stopping at Torremolinos and other centres en route

The colourful façade of the Ayuntamiento (town hall)

Málaga lies protected between the mountains and the sea. It is a busy, friendly city, untouched by much of the conspicuous tourism of the Costa del Sol.

The city's main avenue is the Alameda Principal, attractively shaded by palms and lined with flower stalls and kiosks. The heart of Málaga is north of this street, and east of the Río Guadalmedina, which separates the old town from the new. As soon as you turn off Alameda you will enter a labyrinthine medieval world of narrow, twisting roads with traditional bars and *bodegas* exuding a decidedly local flavour.

Málaga's outstanding features are the old Moorish Alcazaba (➤ 35) and the Castillo de Gibralfaro (➤ 57) which offer magnificent views of the town and bay. Other attractions include the cathedral, Museo Picasso, Museo de Artes y Costumbres Polulares and the Palacio de la Aduana. Among the many small churches don't miss the chapel of the Santuario de la Victoria.

While the cathedral is a focal point from which to start exploring, the main artery of the city centre is the elegant shopping street, Calle Marqués de Larios. On either side are old, narrow streets and small squares where you can browse happily for hours.

The centre is small and many streets are pedestrianised, so it's enjoyable to explore on foot. You can also take a horse-drawn carriage. You will see these lined up by the cathedral in the Paseo del Parque and around the city.

Málaga is famed for its tapas bars. For local atmosphere try one of the *rutas del tapeo* (tapas routes) that cover the area west of Calle Marqués de Larios, around the Calle Nueva. For good seafood restaurants head for the beach suburbs of El Palo or Pedregalejo.

Málaga's La Alcazaba

The Alcazaba fortress has a wonderful sense of antiquity in its rough walls and the maze of terraces, gardens and patios that lead upwards through impressive archways into sunlight.

Rising dramatically above the city are the solid, fortified walls of La Alcazaba, landmark of Málaga. While the fortress dates back to the 700s, most of the structure belongs to the mid-11th century.

From Calle Alcazabilla the way winds up a zig-zag ramp to the Alcazaba, passing through a series of fortified gateways known as the Puerta de la Bóveda, the Puerta de las Columnas, the Torre del Cristo and Puerta de los Cuertos de Granada. The complex includes several delightful patios and some attractively laid out gardens. Terraces offer magnificent views of the town and harbour. A small palace within the inner perimeter is home to the Museo de la Alcazaba, which displays a range of Moorish artefacts recovered from the site and surrounding area.

Just below the entrance to the Alcazaba are the ruins of a Roman amphitheatre. Dating to the second century AD, these remains were uncovered in recent years. Much of the old structure can be seen, with restoration near completion.

INFORMATION

- D2
- Calle Alcazabilla s/n
- 952 22 51 06
- Tue–Sun 8.30–8 (to 7 in winter)
- Inexpensive
- Many nearby
- Centro-Alameda railway station
- Lift up to Alcazaba, entrance behind the town hall (Ayuntamiento)
- Málaga (► 34)

Marbella

INFORMATION

- C2
- 56km west of Málaga
- Wide range of restaurants, many €€€
- Bus station, Avenida del Trapiche s/n 952 76 44 00. Avenida Ricardo Soriano for local services
- Few
- *Carnaval* (pre-Lent); *Feria de la Virgen del Carmen* (16 Jul); *Feria de San Bernabé Patrón* (early Jun); *Feria de San Pedro* (19 Oct)
- Glorieta de la Fontanilla, Paseo Marítimo 952 77 14 42; www.turismomarbella.com; Plaza de los Naranjos 952 82 35 50
- Puerto Banús (➤ 42)

Bonsai Museum

- Parque Arroyo de la Represa
- 952 86 29 26
- Daily 10–1.30, 4.30–8
- Avenida Ricardo Soriano
- Inexpensive Few

Museum of Spanish Contemporary Prints

- Hospital Bazán s/n
- 952 82 50 35
- Mon–Fri 10–2, 5.30–8.30; Sun 10–2
- Avenida Ricardo Soriano
- Few

Marbella – one of the ritziest resorts on the coast – is a playground of the rich and famous, with their luxury yachts and glamorous lifestyles.

Marbella continues to attract the celebrities. The partying goes on but has become less visible as more of the social scene takes place privately. This does not deter many of the visitors, who might still catch sight of a famous face or two.

Celebrities apart, the town's attractions include a thriving commercial centre, the coastal promenade, beach and yacht harbour, and the Casco Antiguo (Old Town, ➤ 37).

The Paseo Marítimo, which stretches far on either side of town, offers an enjoyable stroll along the seafront, with bars and restaurants lining the route. This has been greatly enhanced in recent years by the improvements made to the long stretch of beach, shaded at regular intervals by palm trees. Have a wander around the Puerto Deportivo (yacht harbour), where you can linger over a drink or a meal.

Nearby, the Avenida del Mar, adorned with flowers, fountains and sculptures, leads to the pleasant Parque de la Alameda.

Two museums are worth a visit: the Museo Bonsai, with a delightful collection of Japanese-style miniature trees, and the Museo del Grabado Español Contemporáneo (Museum of Spanish Contemporary Prints) for its exhibitions of works by prominent Spanish artists.

The stretch of coastline between Marbella town and Guadalmina is one of the most attractive parts of the Costa del Sol. It is known as the Golden Mile for its concentration of luxury hotels, magnificent villas, top-class restaurants and golf courses, all amid lush vegetation.

Marbella's Casco Antiguo

The jewel of Marbella is its Casco Antiguo (Old Town), a picturesque maze of narrow streets, pretty squares and whitewashed houses.

Marbella's old quarter is a delightful area in which to browse, with its flower-filled streets, neat little houses and small squares. It is located to the north of Avenida Ramón y Cajal, which cuts through the town. Among its prettiest streets are Remedios, Dolores, Rincón de la Virgen and San Cristóbal, which are noted for the brilliance of their flower displays.

Sooner or later everyone converges on the Plaza de los Naranjos, a charming square lined with neatly pruned orange trees. This is a popular place for a drink or meal out in the open where you can enjoy people watching and life on the streets. In the middle of the square is a bust of a serene-looking King Juan Carlos.

Evidence of the Old Town's Moorish, Christian and Roman past can be seen on many of its buildings. Take a look at the Iglesia de la Incarnación and, above it, the remaining towers of an old Moorish fortress. Also worth noting are the 16th-century Ayuntamiento (town hall) – home of the tourist office, the Casa Consistorial, which boasts a fine Mudéjar entrance, and the Ermita de Nuestro Señor Santiago, Marbella's earliest Christian church.

Worth a glimpse, too, is the attractive little Cofradía del Santo Christo de Amor chapel, at one end of the Plaza de los Naranjos. A stroll through this area is particularly enjoyable in spring when the heady scent of orange blossom fills the air.

INFORMATION

- C2
- Marbella (56km west of Málaga)
- Many restaurants (€–€€€)
- Marbella bus stop, Avenida Ricardo Soriano 21 (Bus station Avenida del Trapiche ☎ 952 76 44 00)
- Few
- Remnants of city walls
- Pre-Lent *Carnaval*; *Feria de San Bernabé* (11–18 Jun)

Mijas

INFORMATION

- D2
- 37km west of Málaga
- Many restaurants (€–€€€)
- Local bus services
- Few
- Benalmádena Pueblo (➤ 50)
- St Anthony's Day (16–17 Jan); *Feria de la Virgen de la Peña* (early Sep); *Romería de Santa Teresa* (end Oct)
- Ayuntamiento, Plaza Virgen de la Peña s/n ☎ 952 48 59 00

With its attractive mountain setting, picturesque narrow streets and white-washed houses, Mijas is a popular excursion from the coast.

As Mijas is only a 20-minute drive from the coast, it makes an ideal destination for a day's excursion. While obviously catering for the tourist, it has still retained much charm. The little town is picturesque, with its white houses, narrow winding streets, flowers and plants. There are magnificent views of the surrounding pine-clad mountains and of the coast below.

On the central square of Plaza de la Virgen you will see the ever-patient donkeys lined up. Adorned with colourful saddles and tassles, they serve as little taxis and can be hired for rides around town. Concerts and fiestas are sometimes held in the square, which centres around a small fountain and is a popular meeting place. There is a large underground car park opposite, which has eased traffic problems.

Near to the square is a neat little park with fine views. Hollowed out from a chunk of rock is a delightful chapel known as the Santuario de la Virgen de la Peña Limosnas. The image of Santa María de la Peña is inside, along with some impressive candlesticks, embroidered garments and other religious relics.

A stroll to the Plaza de la Constitución leads past the Miniature Museum 'Carromato de Max', which has a collection of tiny curios. Up the slope from the Plaza stands the charming little parish church of La Inmaculada Concepción, built mostly in the Mozarabic style. The town's small, rectangular bullring is nearby.

Colourful flowers in the pretty hillside town of Mijas

Nerja

Nerja's attractive setting amid cliffs overlooking rocky coves has earned it a reputation as the jewel of the eastern Costa del Sol.

Nerja lies in a fertile valley of fruit orchards, known mainly for growing peaches and pomegranates. Its name is derived from the old Moorish word *naricha*, meaning 'rich in water'. The town started life as a Moorish farming estate during the 10th century, a centre of the silk and sugar industries. All reminders of its Moorish past and much of the town were destroyed in the earthquake of 1884.

Nerja stands out as one of the most appealing resorts east of Málaga. It retains the charm of its old town, with narrow streets, many pedestrianised, lined with whitewashed houses adorned with flowers and crammed with restaurants. These lead down to Nerja's best-known feature and focal pont, the Balcón de Europa. This curved promontory, lined with palm trees, overlooking the bay is a favoured spot for keen photographers. A series of steps will take you down to the Paseo de los Caribineros and a walkway via several coves to the popular Playa de Burriana. .

Nerja has grown into an internationally popular resort over the years, and so far has managed to escape the sort of development found along much of its neighbouring western coastline. Now linked to Málaga by the Autovía del Mediterraneo, expansion is inevitably on its way, with some new developments to be seen along the seafront.

Some 4km east of Nerja the village of Maro perches on a clifftop above a cove, offering good views of the coastline. The attractive little church of Nuestra Señora de las Maravillas de Maro and the four-tiered aqueduct are particularly interesting.

INFORMATION

- E3
- 52km east of Málaga
- Wide choice of restaurants and bars (€–€€€)
- Bus connections
- Few
- Maro (4km east)
- *Carnaval* (pre-Lent); *Semana Santa* (Easter); *Cruces de Mayo* (3 May); *Fiesta de la Virgen del Carmen* (16 Jul); *Feria de Nerja* (13 Oct)
- Puerta del Mar 4 ☎ 952 52 15 31; www.nerja.org

One of Nerja's coves

Nerja's Cuevas de Nerja

INFORMATION

- E2
- 4km east of Nerja
- 952 52 95 20
- Daily 10–2, 4–8 (6.30 in winter)
- Inexpensive
- Restaurant (€€)
- Occasional buses, but best reached by car
- None
- Nerja (➤ 39)
- Summer concerts and ballet performances
- In Nerja (➤ 39)

Below: *dramatic lighting at the Cuevas de Nerja*

These caverns contain spectacular stalactites and stalagmites. Prehistoric man painted pictures on the rocks here thousands of years ago.

The limestone caves were discovered by chance in 1959 by a group of boys who were out and about exploring. Beyond the first grotto, great caverns revealed a wonderful world of stalactites and stalagmites, some wall paintings and various items such as stone tools and fragments of pottery. Investigations by experts show that the area must have been inhabited by man more than 20,000 years ago. A group of sculptures near the entrance to the caves honours the boys who made the discovery.

The rock paintings of horses, deer, goats and dolphins are not open for public viewing, but photographs of them are on display, together with some of the artefacts found here. For the tourist, however, the main attraction lies in the magnificent rock formations, which are enhanced by special lighting effects.

The first chamber provides a magnificent setting for concerts, which are held here as part of an annual summer festival. The next cavern is called the Hall of Ghosts after a strange shroud-like figure which appears in the stone. The most impressive, however, is the huge Hall of Cataclysms, which features the tallest column of its kind rising mightily from the mass of stalactites.

Parque Natural El Torcal de Antequera

El Torcal and its spectacular rock formations, 13km south of Antequera, is one of the most remarkable of Andalucía's Natural Parks.

The Parque Natural El Torcal de Antequera covers 1,171ha of grey limestone rocks and boulders that have been weathered with time to form the most amazing shapes.

The name *Torcal* derives from the word for 'twist' and aptly sums up the maze of narrow vegetation-filled gullies and ravines winding among the towering reefs and pillars of rock. From the visitor's car park there are several waymarked circular walking routes through the labyrinth. The shortest of these routes, around 1.5km, tends to be crowded. For long walks you must be accompanied by an official guide – book in advance. An early morning or late afternoon visit is recommended.

The dense undergrowth is formed from holm oak, hawthorn, maple and elder. Ivy clings to the rock faces. Countless flowering plants include saxifrage, peony, rock buttercup, rock rose, thistle and numerous species of orchid. El Torcal's general isolation supports a rich birdlife that includes the great grey shrike, vultures and eagles, as well as numerous small perching birds. There is a good chance of spotting the harmless but fierce-looking ocellated lizard, the largest lizard in Europe.

A reception centre at the entrance to El Torcal has an exhibition and audio-visual display with excellent information about the geology and wildlife of the area. Exhibits are labelled in Spanish only. A short path leads from near the reception centre to the Mirador El Ventanillo, a spectacular viewpoint.

INFORMATION

- D1
- 13km south of Antequera
- 952 03 13 89
- Reception centre: Tue–Sun 10–2, 4–6
- Cafe (€€)
- Few
- Antequera (➤ 25)

Twisted boulders in the Parque Natural El Torcal

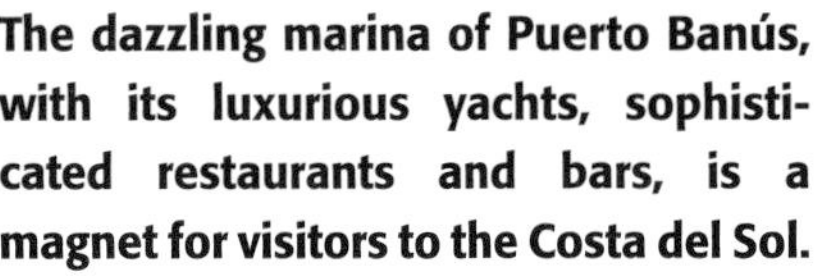

Puerto Banús

INFORMATION

- C2
- 64km west of Málaga, 6km west of Marbella
- Many bars and restaurants (€€–€€€)
- From Marbella and San Pedro de Alcántara
- Few
- San Pedro de Alcántara (➤ 53)
- Regattas, sailing and fishing competitions
- Avenida Principal s/n
  ☎ 952 11 38 30 (summer only)

Apartments nestle between the beach and the mountains in this exclusive resort

The dazzling marina of Puerto Banús, with its luxurious yachts, sophisticated restaurants and bars, is a magnet for visitors to the Costa del Sol.

A stay on the Costa del Sol would be incomplete without a visit to Puerto Banús, one of the coast's most famous attractions. Created by the promoter José Banús in 1968, it was one of Spain's first village-type marina developments.

Backed by the mountains, a ring of brilliant white apartment houses surrounds the marina, which is filled with craft of all sizes, from mega yachts to small sailing boats. A feature of Banús is the Arab-built complex of luxury apartments, on the right as you enter the port. With its opulent marble façade and gleaming turrets, the inspiration could have been taken straight from the *Arabian Nights*.

Around the port is a string of cafés, bars and restaurants, along with boutiques and gift shops. While restaurants on the quayside are the places in which to be seen, you'll sometimes get better value from the small restaurants tucked away up flights of stairs in the streets behind it. During the season the quayside is thronged with people who come to see or be seen – it is a great place for celebrity-spotting: The Salduba Pub and Sinatra Bar are best for this pastime.

At night the smart restaurants, slick piano bars and nightclubs fill up with the chichi set. While the glamour of its earlier days may have dimmed a little, Banús still rates as one of the coast's star attractions.

Ronda

Ronda is renowned for its spectacular setting. This, along with legends of bandits, adds a certain mystique that continues to attract visitors.

A mighty split in the El Tajo gorge, spanned by the Puente Nuevo (▶ 44), divides the town into Old Ronda (La Ciudad) and the newer part, El Mercadillo. Most monuments of note are in the old town, which retains Moorish influences. These include the imposing church of Santa María la Mayor, the Minaret of San Sebastián, the Palacio de Mondragón and the Casa del Gigante, the Palacio del Marqués de Salvatierra and the gardens of the Casa del Rey Moro. The Museo Lara (science and history) and Museo del Bandolero (legends of local bandits) are also worth a visit. The café-lined Plaza del Socorro is the focal point of the newer part of town, Ronda's main shopping centre, with magnificent views from the gardens of the Alameda del Tajo nearby.

The bullring, near the Puente Nuevo, was built in 1785 and is the oldest in Spain. The rules of modern bullfighting were laid down here by Francisco Romero, whose grandson Pedro Romero went on to become one of Spain's most famous matadors. The bullring, now owned by Antonio Ordoñez, another of the greats, is used only for special fiestas. The museum behind the ring contains glittering costumes, gear and a wealth of photographs.

Ronda is a city with a cultural past. Writer Ernest Hemingway and actor Orson Welles, were keen followers of the bullfight. Both spent much time down here and each of them formed a close friendship with Ordoñez. By his own request, the ashes of Orson Welles are scattered over the bullfighter's nearby ranch.

Some 20km southwest of Ronda is the Cueva de la Pileta (Pileta Cave), with prehistoric rock paintings believed to be 25,000 years old.

INFORMATION

- C1
- 118km northwest of Málaga
- Many restaurants (€–€€€)
- From Algeciras, Málaga (via Bobadilla)
- Few
- Pedro Romero Festival (▶ 22)
- Plaza de España 1
  952 18 71 19; www.turismoderonda.es

Cueva de la Pileta

- 20km southwest of Ronda
- 952 16 73 43
- Daily 10–1, 4–6; tours last about one hour
- Moderate
- Few

Houses perch on the edge of the spectacular El Tajo gorge.

Ronda's Puente Nuevo

INFORMATION

- C1
- 118km northwest of Málaga
- Many restaurants in Ronda (€–€€€)
- From Algeciras, Cádiz, Málaga (via Torremolinos, Marbella, San Pedro) and Sevilla
- Ronda (➤ 43), Cueva de la Pileta (➤ 43)
- At Ronda

The Puente Nuevo is a popular tourist attraction

This spectacular 18th-century bridge has become the symbol of Ronda. It spans the towering El Tajo gorge, through which the Río Guadalevín flows, and provides visitors with breathtaking views.

Ronda has long associations with painters and writers, for many of whom the town has held a deep fascination. The scene of Ronda perched on the clifftop and, in particular, its spectacular bridge has been the subject of countless paintings and photographs.

The River Guadalevín divides Ronda in two. Linking old Ronda with the 'new town' is the Puente Nuevo (New Bridge), which spans the river's deep gorge (El Tajo).

Work began on the bridge in 1751 and finished in 1793. The bridge stands a full 96m above the gorge at its highest and narrowest point. The unfortunate architect fell to his death from a basket lowered to allow him to inspect the building work.

The dramatic views from the bridge, combined with the many attractions of the old town and its historical interest (➤ 43), make Ronda a top excursion for visitors staying along the coast.

Sevilla

Sevilla generates a style and romance all of its own. Andalucía's capital and most fashionable city, it is home to great art and magnificent monuments, as well as streets full of elegant shops, bars and restaurants.

Sevilla, Spain's fourth largest city, is dominated by the minaret tower of La Giralda and the great cathedral it adjoins (➤ 47). Various cultures have left their mark here, from the Romans to the Moors and the Christians. In the 16th and 17th centuries Sevilla became the most important port in Spain. During this period, often described as Spain's Golden Age, the Sevilla school of painters brought great prestige to the city.

Sevilla is a city to explore on foot, and the cathedral is a good starting point. The medieval quarter of the Barrio Santa Cruz, nearby, is a delightful maze of narrow streets and whitewashed houses adorned with wrought-iron balconies, decked with flowers.

A stroll around Sevilla reveals mansions, squares and lovely parks, such as the Parque de María Luisa, the Murillo gardens and those of the Reales Alcázares (➤ 48). The large Plaza de España contains a tiny canal, decorated bridges and fountains. An imposing crescent has ceramic tiles depicting Spain's provincial capitals. Over the bridge is the Triana area, home of the gypsy population. Alternative ways of getting around are by 'SevillaTour' buses, or in style by horse-drawn carriage.

Well known as the setting for *Carmen* and other famous operas, Sevilla has long had a romantic image. In the spring, when the heady scent of orange blossom gives the city a special atmosphere, the celebrations of *Semana Santa* (Holy Week) and the exuberant *Feria de Sevilla* take place (➤ 22).

INFORMATION

- See fold-out map
- 219km northwest of Málaga
- Many restaurants and tapas bars
- Bus stations: Prado de San Sebastián ☎ 954 41 71 11 and Plaza de Armas ☎ 954 90 77 37
- Few
- Estación de FFCC Santa Justa, Avenida Kansas City s/n ☎ 954 54 02 02
- *Semana Santa* (Easter); *Feria de Sevilla* (2 weeks after Easter); *Corpus Christi; Fiesta de la Virgen de los Reyes* (15 Aug)
- Avenida de la Constitución 21 B ☎ 954 22 14 04; www.turismosevilla.org

The internal entrance to Sevilla's bullring

Sevilla's Casa de Pilatos

INFORMATION

- Plaza Pilatos 1
- 954 22 52 98
- Daily 9–6
- C1, C2, C3, C4
- Good
- Ground floor free; upper floors moderate (free Tue pm)

La Casa de Pilatos is a glorious celebration of the Mudéjar style mixed with the most Italianate features. To have such sustained Mudéjar design in one building is a delight.

This 16th-century private mansion is one of Sevilla's great sights. Built in 1519, the house was said to be a copy of Pontius Pilate's house in Jerusalem, but there is no real evidence to confirm this.

One of La Casa de Pilatos' ornate patios

Combining the Mudéjar, Gothic and Renaissance architectural styles, the entire building is adorned with delicate carving, tilework and wooden coffered ceilings. The *azulejos* tiling is outstanding, and the patios, arcades, archways, stairways and richly furnished salons are all superb. A grand staircase leads to the upper floors, which contain a collection of art. The adjoining gardens may also be visited.

There is hardly a better self-contained complex of late medieval style in all of Andalucía. La Casa de Pilatos is one of the best places to get a feel for the subtle complexities of this delightful and intriguing architectural style.

24

Sevilla's La Giralda y La Catedral

The minaret known as La Giralda is a symbol of Sevilla. It rises proudly above the great Cathedral, the third largest in Europe and among the continent's most visited monuments.

These are stunning buildings by any measure, and they can get very crowded.

The 98m-high brick tower of La Giralda was built in the 12th century as the minaret of the former Great Mosque. In 1565 a section with 25 bells was added and topped with a bronze statue representing Faith, which acts as a giralda (weather vane). From the belfry there are magnificent views over the city and beyond. Take care, though, there are 34 ramps to the top!

The grand cathedral was built in the Gothic style, with some Renaissance influences. The interior is awe-inspiring with its vast size and richness of decoration. Gothic columns supporting massive arches reach up to the great heights of the vaulted ceiling.

A handsome 16th-century plateresque grille in the Sanctuary encloses an immense golden Gothic altarpiece, said to be the largest altar in the world. Started by the Flemish artist Dancart in 1482, it took almost a hundred years to complete the 45 tableaux depicting the life of Jesus and Mary. Above the 16th-century shrine stands an image of the Virgen de la Sede.

The choirstalls are fine examples of flamboyant Gothic. Notable also is the Capilla Real (Royal Chapel), completed in 1575. On either side are the tombs of King Alfonso X (the Wise) and his mother, Beatrice of Swabia. In the south transept lies the ornate tomb of Christopher Columbus, whose body lay here for a time after it was transported from Cuba.

INFORMATION

- Plaza Virgen de los Reyes
- 954 21 49 71
- Jul–Aug Mon–Sat 9.30–3.30, Sun 2.30–6; rest of year Mon–Sat 11–5, Sun 2–6
- Moderate; Sun free
- Many restaurants nearby
- RENFE station
- Few
- Sevilla (➤ 45)

La Giralda soars over the city

Sevilla's Reales Alcázares

INFORMATION

- Plaza del Triunfo
- 954 50 23 23
- Tue–Sat 9:30–7, Sun 9:30–5
- Moderate
- C1, C2, C3, C4
- Few
- Go early if possible. Restrictions on visitor numbers during busy periods can result in queues

The Royal Palaces of Sevilla are a marvel. The centrepiece, the Palacio Mudéjar del Rey Don Pedro, is a superb example of Mudéjar art.

After Sevilla fell to Christian forces in 1248, the Spanish king Pedro the Cruel reshaped and rebuilt much of the city's original Alcázar in Mudéjar style. It is this version that survives at the heart of the present complex, in spite of many restorations and often clumsy additions made by later monarchs.

Highlights of the Alcázares include the Chapel of the Navigators, where Isabella of Castile masterminded the conquest of the Spanish Americas. The room's coffered wooden ceiling, a classic example of *artesonado* style, is studded with golden stars. Inside the palace proper is the Patio of the Maidens, with fine stucco work and *azulejos* tiling. Beyond lies the Salón de Carlos V, with another superb *artesonado* ceiling and then the Alcázar's finest room, the Salon of the Ambassadors, crowned by a glorious dome of wood in green, red and gold and with a Moorish arcade.

Adjoining the main palace are the dull and cavernous chambers of the Palacio de Carlos V, added by that insatiable intruder upon fine buildings, the Habsburg Emperor. These lead to the serene gardens of the Alcázares. An arc of water from a high faucet crashes spectacularly into a pool where a bronze statue of Mercury stands in front of a rusticated façade: the Gallery of the Grotesque. The rest of the gardens make a pleasant walk before you emerge into the Patio de las Banderas, with Sevilla's mighty cathedral (➤ 47) beckoning ahead.

Strolling past Sevilla's Reales Alcázares

COSTA DEL SOL's best

White Towns

PUEBLOS BLANCOS
Dazzling white towns and villages on mountain tops are a familiar part of the Andalusian landscape. The famous *Pueblos Blancos*, or White Towns of Andalucía, are located in the area between Ronda, Sevilla, Cádiz and Algeciras. As well as the whitewashed houses that give them their name, they all have steep, narrow streets, often leading up to a castle.
Ronda is a good starting point for a tour of the White Towns. The route will lead you through rugged mountain landscapes where Moors fought Christians and legends about bandits abound.
As well as the famous White Towns, this section features other places that possess the features of a typical Andalusian town.

Scenic Cómpeta

In the Top 25

1 **ALMUÑÉCAR (➤ 24)**
2 **ANTEQUERA (➤ 25)**
3 **CASARES (➤ 26)**
7 **FRIGILIANA (➤ 30)**
15 **MIJAS (➤ 38)**

BENALMÁDENA PUEBLO
Benalmádena Pueblo's origins are thought to date back to Phoenician times. This is a charming little village of narrow twisting streets and whitewashed houses. With attractive views of the coast and surrounding landscapes, it offers a rural atmosphere. The Museo Arqueológico contains some pre-Columbian exhibits, along with artefacts from Roman and early Iberian times.
D2 3km west of Arroyo de la Miel Variety of restaurants and bars Few Tivoli World Amusement Park (➤ 58) Local fair (15 Aug); *Feria de San Juan* (24 Jun) at nearby Arroyo de la Miel

CÓMPETA
Way up in the mountains of La Axarquia, the region east of Málaga, is the small picturesque town of Cómpeta, which can be reached by taking the road leading inland from Torrox-Costa. Cómpeta is noted for its attractive setting, perched on a mountain ridge surrounded by vineyards. The town is made up of a cluster of whitewashed houses and winding streets. On the main square stands the baroque Iglesia de la Asunción, with an impressive bell tower. Cómpeta has a community of foreign residents, some of whom are involved with craft industries. A big attraction is the lively wine festival, held each year in August.
E2 51km east of Málaga Several restaurants (€–€€) Local services Few Nerja (➤ 39) *Noche del Vino* (15 Aug) Plaza Almijira s/n 952 55 33 01

GAUCÍN
As you approach Gaucín you will be faced by a host of whitewashed houses, topped by red roofs, spread out beneath the rocks. The old Moorish fortress, Castillo de Aguila (Eagle's Castle), now partly restored, stands high above the village, forming a silhouette against the backdrop of mountains. From this vantage point there are magnificent views across the valley of the Guadiaro river, reaching out to the coastline as far as the Rock of Gibraltar. The village is delightful and abounds with colourful flowers and plants. Its narrow streets and one-way system are not conducive to driving, however, and the place is best explored on foot. The daily fish market is always a lively event.

B2 120km west of Málaga Several restaurants Local bus services Few Casares (➤ 26) *Romería San Juan* (23 Jun); *Feria Virgen de las Nieves* (second week Aug); *Fiesta de Santo Niño* (8, 9 and 10 Sep) Calle Fuente 91, Casares 952 89 41 26

SALOBREÑA

Some 13km east of Almuñécar is the attractive little town of Salobreña, now within that stretch of coast known as the Costa Tropical. It lies a short distance from the sea among fruit orchards and sugarcane plantations. Salobreña has a cluster of whitewashed houses sprawling up the hill, dominated by the old Moorish *alcázar* known as El Capricho. The castle has been well restored and offers magnificent views of the coast, surrounding countryside and the beautiful peaks of the Sierra Nevada. Also worth a visit is the 16th-century church of Nuestra Señora del Rosario, built on the site of an old mosque. Much of Salobreña's charm lies in the fact that it remains relatively unspoilt, with few hotels and restaurants. It provides a good gateway to Granada, however, and can receive quite an influx of visitors, especially at weekends. From here it is only 4km further along the coast to Motril, a commercial centre for sugarcane. Take a look at the Sanctuary of Our Lady of the Head, at the top of the hill. Enthusiasts can enjoy the golf course here.

F3 93km east of Málaga Choice of restaurants (€–€€€) Bus connections Few Almuñécar (13km west, ➤ 24) *Semana Santa* (Easter); *Fiesta de San Juan y San Pedro* (end Jul); *Fiesta de Nuestra Señora del Rosario* (early Oct) Plaza de Goya s/n 958 61 03 14

VÉLEZ-MÁLAGA

The small town of Vélez-Málaga lies 5km inland from Torre del Mar, surrounded by subtropical vegetation. Capital of La Axarquía, it is the centre of an agricultural region known for its production of strawberries and for its vineyards, which produce the muscatel grapes from which the famous Málaga wines are made. It is also a centre for the processing of olive oil and sugarcane. If you are here on a Thursday, wander around the weekly market. The town is crowned by a 13th-century Moorish castle and there are good views of the surrounding countryside from up here. The oldest part of the town, the Arrabal de San Sebastián, is a picturesque area of narrow streets. The 15th-century church of Santa María la Mayor was the first building erected by the Christians, following their victory over the Moors here in 1487.

E2 34km east of Málaga Many restaurants (€–€€€) Bus connections Few Nerja (➤ 39) Avenida de Andalucía 119 952 54 11 04

Top: *the view from Salobreña's castle*
Above: *Vélez-Málaga, seen from the town's castle*

Beach Resorts

TOP BEACHES

The Costa del Sol's best beaches include:
Bajondillo, Torremolinos
La Carihuela, Torremolinos
Santa Ana, Benalmádena
La Vibora, between Benalmádena and Fuengirola
Playa de Los Boliches, Los Boliches
Playa de Fuengirola, Fuengirola
La Cala, between Fuengirola and Marbella
Fontanilla, Marbella
La Rada, Estepona
Cala de Maro, east of Nerja

Top: *Benalmádena's marina*
Above: *the sweeping curve of Marbella's beach*

In the Top 25

11 **MÁLAGA (► 34)**
13 **MARBELLA (► 36)**
16 **NERJA (► 39)**

BENALMÁDENA COSTA

Benalmádena Costa is, in effect, an extension of Torremolinos. It covers a long stretch of coast lined with the type of high-rise apartment blocks that characterise this section of the Costa del Sol. Puerto Deportivo is one of the coast's newer marina developments and has become a major attraction in the area.
D2 20km west of Málaga Numerous restaurants and bars (€–€€€) Connections Railway station Benalmádena–Arroyo de la Miel Few Sea Life Centre (► 58) *Virgen del Carmen fiesta* (16 Jul) Avenida Antonio Machado 16 952 44 12 95; www.benalmadena.com

ESTEPONA

Estepona is another of the Costa del Sol's fast developing resorts and offers a long beach, seafront promenade, a marina and at least three golf courses. It is also a good centre for sailing and windsurfing. This former fishing village retains a large fleet. Wander down to the port early in the morning and watch the fresh catch being sold at the fish market.The old town dates back to Roman and Moorish times. The focal point is the charming little square of the Plaza de las Flores, entered by four archways of trees. Take a look at the church on Plaza del Reloj and go down the steps to the Mercado Municipal, a covered market. Above the town are old castle ruins.
B2 82km west of Málaga Few *Fiesta de San Isidro* (15 May); local festival (early Jul); *Fiesta de Virgen del Carmen* (16 Jul) Avenida San Lorenzo 1 952 80 09 13; www.estepona.es

FUENGIROLA

Fuengirola has a long sweep of beach, offering all kinds of watersports, an attractive yacht club and marina, along with an extended promenade, the Paseo Marítimo, which links Fuengirola, Los Boliches and Carvajal. A lively meeting place in the old part of town is the Plaza de la Constitución, dominated by Fuengirola's main church. The old fishermen's district of Santa Fé has character and high above the town is the old Moorish Castle, Castillo de Sohail; walk up here for excellent views of the coast.
D3 29km west of Málaga Corner Ave Ramón y Cajal and Calle Alfonso XIII RENFE station at Ave Jesús Santos Rein (half-hourly service to Málaga) Good *Fiesta de la Virgen del Carmen* (16 Jul) in Los Boliches; *Romería* (late Sep) from Fuengirola; *Feria del Rosario* (7 Oct) Paseo Jesús Santos Rein 6 952 46 74 57; www.fuengirola.org

SAN PEDRO DE ALCÁNTARA

San Pedro de Alcántara has undergone a facelift in recent years. The Calle Marqués del Duero, shaded by orange trees and palms, and lined with shops and cafés, leads up the hill to the small square of Plaza de la Iglesia, with a fountain. Next to the town hall is San Pedro's parish church, its white façade framed by two palm trees. Three archaeological sites nearby are worth exploring: the 6th-century Visigoth Basílica de Vega del Mar, the 1st-century Villa Romana de Río Verde, and Las Bovedas, remains of Roman thermal baths.

C2 70km west of Málaga Few Avenida Marqués del Duero, 69 952 78 52 52

TORRE DEL MAR

Torre del Mar is the beach resort of Vélez-Málaga (► 51). It consists primarily of a long beach lined with a string of high-rise apartment blocks. The extended esplanade follows the coast to the Marina of Caleta de Vélez, with its lively cafés.

E2 30km east of Málaga Choice of restaurants and bars (€–€€€) Bus connections Few Fiestas at Vélez-Málaga Avenida de Andalucía 52 952 54 11 04

TORREMOLINOS

Torremolinos lies on the most developed part of the coast. Calle San Miguel is the main artery of the town, lined with boutiques and shops. The Cuesta del Tajo, at the end of San Miguel, leads down a flight of steps through the fishing district of El Bajondillo. Down at the bottom is the beach of El Bajondillo. To the left are the beaches of Playamar and Los Alamos. To the right, beyond the Castillo de Santa Clara, lie the beach areas of La Carihuela and Montemar. The seafront promenade, Paseo Marítimo, now continues as far as Benalmádena Costa (► 52). The walk to the old fishing village of La Carihuela offers pleasant sea views. The village has picturesque houses and a reputation for excellent fish restaurants.

D2 12km west of Málaga Half-hourly to Málaga (25 minutes) and Fuengirola Few *Carnaval* (pre-Lent); *Feria de Verdiales* (Mar); Easter; *Fiesta de la Virgen del Carmen* (16 Jul); *Día del Turista* (early Sep); *Feria de San Miguel* (late Sep); *Romería de San Miguel* (Sun, late Sep) Ayuntamiento, Plaza Blas Infante 1 952 37 95 12; www.ayto-torremolinos.org

TORROX COSTA

Torrox Costa's long stretch of beach is backed with modern apartment blocks, sympathetically designed with reflections of the Moorish style of architecture. Some 4km inland lies the attractive old town of Torrox.

E2 47km east of Málaga Bus connections Few Centro Internacional, bloque 79 952 53 02 25

THE TIP OF EUROPE

To stand on the Punta de Tarifa is to be at the southernmost point of mainland Europe, with the coast of the African continent only 14km away. On the fringe of the Costa del Sol, Tarifa has a totally different flavour about it, which in itself makes a visit worthwhile. The town has played an important role in the history of the Iberian peninsula. With its dazzling white houses and maze of narrow, winding streets, it retains a distinctive Moorish look. Tarifa is blessed by a long expanse of sandy beach backed by pine trees. This marks the meeting point of the Mediterranean and the Atlantic and the strong winds which sweep across the sand create excellent conditions for kite-and-windsurfing in the bay.

A3 21km west of Algeciras

A café on the beach at Torremolinos

Museums

MUSEO PICASSO

The Picasso Museum is housed in the 16th-century Palacio de Buenavista. The museum has a permanent collection of more than 200 of Picasso's works. The selection of paintings, drawings, sculptures, engravings and pottery illustrates the breadth of Picasso's long and prolific career as an artist of extraordinary talent. Also on display, on the lower ground floor, are some Phoenician and Roman remains, uncovered during the renovations of the palace.
✉ Palacio de Buenavista, Calle San Augustín 8 ☎ 902 44 33 77 ◷ Tue–Thu 10–8, Fri & Sat 10–9 ✋ Moderate ♿ Wheelchairs upon request

CASA MUSEO GARCÍA LORCA, FUENTE VAQUEROS

This was the home of playwright and poet Federico García Lorca, who was born in Fuente Vaqueros in 1898. Lorca, who spent much time in nearby Granada, was known for the sensitivity of his poetry and the powerful drama of his plays, such as *Yerma*, *Blood Wedding* and *The House of Bernarda Alba*. He was assassinated during the Spanish Civil War.
✚ F1 ✉ 17km west of Granada ✉ Calle poeta García Lorca, 4 ☎ 958 51 64 53 ◷ Tue–Sun 10–1, 4–8 (winter 4–6). Tours hourly ✋ Inexpensive ♿ Few

CASA NATAL DE PICASSO, MÁLAGA

Spain's celebrated painter, Pablo Ruiz Picasso, was born in 1881 in the corner house of an elegant block on Plaza de la Merced. His birthplace was declared a historic-artistic monument in 1983, and in 1991 it became the headquarters of the Pablo Ruiz Picasso Foundation. There is an exhibition covering two floors that includes early sketches by the artist, plus sculptures, photos of Picasso and his family, and memorabilia, including the artist's christening robe. Picasso began to paint here, helped by his father, an art teacher, who recognised his son's talent.
✚ D2 ✉ Plaza de la Merced 15 ☎ 952 06 02 15 ◷ Mon–Sat 11–2, 5–8, Sun 11–2 ✋ Inexpensive 🍴 Many nearby (€–€€€) 🚆 Centro-Alameda railway station ♿ Few

MONASTERIO DE LA CARTUJA, GRANADA

This former Carthusian Monastery, dating back to the 16th century, has paintings and sculpture.
✚ F1 ✉ Paseo de la Cartuja ☎ 958 16 1932 ◷ Apr–Oct, Mon–Sat 10–1, 4–8; Nov–Mar daily 10–1, 3.30–6.30 ✋ Inexpensive (free Sun)

MUSEO ARQUEOLÓGICO, GRANADA

The museum is housed in the Casa Castril, an elegant Renaissance palace, noted for its delicately carved plateresque doorway. It has a fine collection of ceramics from Roman and Moorish times and some superb Egyptian vases unearthed in the region.
✚ F1 ✉ Carrera del Darro 41 ☎ 958 22 56 40 ◷ Apr–Oct Wed–Sat 9–8, Tue 2.30–8, Sun 9–2.30; Nov–Mar Wed–Sat 9–6, Tue 2.30–6. Sun 9–2.30 ✋ Inexpensive (EU citizens free) ♿ Few

MUSEO ARQUEOLÓGICO, SEVILLA

Housed in the Renaissance palace built for the 1929 Ibero-America Exhibition, this museum displays objects from prehistory and the Moorish culture. Outstanding is the Carombolo Treasure.
✚ See fold-out map ✉ Plaza de América ☎ 954 23 24 01 ◷ Wed–Sat 9–8, Tue 3–8, Sun, public hols 9–2 ✋ Inexpensive (EU citizens free) ♿ Few

MUSEO ARQUEOLÓGICO, CÓRDOBA

This museum, in the attractive 16th-century Palacio de los Páez, has a fine collection of objects, ranging from prehistoric to Roman and Moorish times.
See fold-out map Plaza Jerónimo Páez 7 957 47 40 11 Wed–Sat 9–8, Tue 2.30–8.30, Sun, public hols 9–2.30 Few Inexpensive (EU citizens free)

MUSEO DE ARTES Y COSTUMBRES POPULARES, MÁLAGA

This charming museum, in a former 17th-century inn, displays artefacts from the rural and seagoing life of old Málaga province. It gives an insight into the past ways and customs of the people of the region. Agricultural items, a fishing boat and house interiors are on the ground floor, while the first floor has costumes, ceramics, tiles and religious relics.
D2 Pasillo de Santa Isabel 10 952 21 71 37 Summer Mon–Fri 10–1, 5–8, Sat 10–12; rest of year Mon–Fri 10–1.30, 4–7, Sat 10–12. Closed public hols Inexpensive Few

MUSEO DE BELLAS ARTES, CÓRDOBA

This fine arts museum contains paintings and sculptures by some of Spain's great masters, including Goya, Luis Maroles and Alonso.
See fold-out map Plaza de Potro, 1 957 47 33 45 Wed–Sat 9–8.30, Tue 2.30–8.30, Sun, public hols 9–2.30 Few Inexpensive (EU citizens free)

MUSEO DE BELLAS ARTES, SEVILLA

This museum, in the former Convento de la Merced, contains a splendid collection of paintings and sculpture, ceramics and weapons. Room V has works by masters including Zurbarán and Murillo.
See fold-out map Plaza Museo 9 954 22 07 90 Wed–Sat 9–8, Tue 3–8, Sun, public hols 9–2 Inexpensive (EU citizens free) Few

MUSEO MUNICIPAL TAURINO, CÓRDOBA

The Municipal Bullfighting Museum, in an elegant 16th-century mansion, has a fascinating display of memorabilia relating to some of Córdoba's most famous bullfighters, including the legendary Manolete.
See fold-out map Plaza Maimónides 5 957 20 10 56 Tue–Sat 10–2, 4.30–6.30; Sun, public hols 9.30–2.30 Moderate (free Fri) Few

TORRE DE LA CALAHORRA, CÓRDOBA

Housed in the 14th-century Moorish fortress across the river, the Museo Histórico traces the history of Córdoba at the height of its golden era.
See fold-out map Puente Romano 957 29 39 29 Daily 10–6 Moderate None

DREAMS

The Austrian romantic poet Rainer María Rilke went to Ronda in 1913 to recuperate from an illness. He wrote of the town: 'Everywhere I sought the dream of a city and at last I have found it.'
His room at the Reina Victoria Hotel has been kept much as it was and preserved as a tiny museum. A key may be requested at reception if you want to visit the room, which contains some photographs and verses written by Rilke during his stay. His sensitivity is well portrayed in the statue that stands in the garden.

The Torre de la Calahorra, Córdoba

Churches

In the Top 25

5 **CÓRDOBA'S LA MEZQUITA (➤ 28)**
10 **GRANADA'S CAPILLA REAL (➤ 33)**
24 **SEVILLA'S LA CATEDRAL (➤ 47)**

TERM OF ENDEARMENT

While original plans for Málaga's cathedral allowed for two towers, lack of funds resulted in the completion of only one. This gave rise to the name by which the cathedral is affectionately referred to, La Manquita, loosely interpreted as 'the little one-armed woman.'

Top: *the lonely tower of Málaga's cathedral*
Above: *Málaga's Iglesia del Sagrario has an impressive Renaissance high altar*

CATEDRAL, GRANADA

The cathedral was begun in 1528 on the orders of the Catholic Monarchs. Construction was under the great master Diego de Siloé, and continued after his death in 1528. It features a magnificent Capilla Real (Royal Chapel) and has a notable rotunda, with some fine paintings by Alonso Cano, a native of Granada.
F1 Gran Vía 5 958 22 29 59 Mon–Sat 10.30–1.30, 4–7, Sun 4–7 Inexpensive Few

CATEDRAL, MÁLAGA

Málaga's cathedral gets something of a bad press, due perhaps to its lack of a companion for its solitary tower. Another tower was planned originally, but was never constructed. The cathedral has a strong visual appeal, however, its dark, worn stonework making a pleasing contrast to the more modern buildings that crowd round it. Inside, there is much Gothic gloom, in heavily marbled surroundings with numerous attractive side chapels competing for attention. The *coro*, or choir, is the cathedral's great glory. Its fine mahogany and cedar wood stalls are embellished by carved statues of 40 saints. The adjoining church, the Iglesia del Sagrario, has a plateresque doorway and a Renaissance high altar that will take your breath away.
D2 Calle Molina Larios, s/n 952 21 59 17 Mon–Sat 10–6.45. Closed public hols Inexpensive None Centro-Alameda railway station Few

IGLESIA DEL SANTO CRISTO DE LA SALUD, MÁLAGA

The interior of this 17th-century church is a real gem. Note the brilliant altarpiece and beautifully decorated cupola. The church also contains the tomb of architect Pedro de la Mena.
D2 Calle Compañia 952 21 34 56 Free

SANTUARIO DE LA VICTORIA, MÁLAGA

The church was erected in 1487 on the site where the Catholic Monarchs pitched their tents during the siege of that year. A major feature is the magnificent retable which rises above the main altar. High up, amid a flourish of exuberant ornamentation, is a small *camerín* (chapel) containing a statue of the Madonna and Child (reached by stairs at the far end of the church).
D2 Plaza del Santuario 952 25 26 47 Tue–Fri 10–12, 4.30–7, Sat 10–12 Free Centro-Alameda railway station Few

Palaces & Castles

In the Top 25

CASTILLO DE GIBRALFARO, MÁLAGA

Right above the Alcazaba (➤ 35) stands the Castillo de Gibralfaro, crowning the hill of the same name. Yusef I of Granada built the castle at the beginning of the 14th century on a former Phoenician site. It was once the site of a lighthouse, from which its name derived – *gebel-faro* (rock of the lighthouse). This was once the scene of a three-month siege by the citizens of Málaga against the Catholic Monarchs, Ferdinand and Isabella. Eventually hunger forced the citizens to surrender, and Ferdinand occupied the site while his queen took up residence in the town. All that remains today of this historic monument is a series of solid ramparts, rising majestically among dense woods of pines and eucalyptus. Although it can be reached on foot from the Alcazaba, it's a safer bet to visit the castle direct, by bus, car, even by horse and carriage. The nearby Parador Málaga-Gibralfaro offers panoramic views of the city and harbour, with landmarks such as the cathedral and bullring clearly visible.

D2 Gibralfaro Mountain 952 22 20 43 Daily 9–6 Inexpensive Parador nearby Bus 35 None

The Castillo de Gibralfaro, Málaga

PALACIO DE LA ADUANA, MÁLAGA

The Hall of Columns (Salón de Columnas) in this neoclassical former Customs House, which was on the waterfront until the construction of the Paseo del Parque, now exhibits part of the art collection from the Museum of Fine Arts (Museo de Bellas Artes). The exhibitions and displays are changed at regular intervals. Eventually the whole collection may be rehoused in a new location.

D2 Paseo del Parque 952 21 36 80 Tue 3–8, Wed–Fri 9–8, Sat, Sun 9–3 Free Few

ALCÁZAR DE LOS REYES CRISTIANOS, CÓRDOBA

This Mudéjar-style palace was begun by King Alfonso XI in the early 14th century. Outstanding Roman mosaics, the old Moorish courtyard and baths still remain. This was once the residence of the Catholic Kings, and a one-time Moorish prison.

See fold-out map Campo Santo de los Mártires 957 42 01 51 Tue–Sat 4.30–6.30; Sun, public hols 9.30–2.30 Moderate (free Fri) Few

Children's Activities

FUN FOR KIDS

Spaniards are known for their fondness for children, who can expect to be treated with courtesy and made to feel welcome. There is plenty to amuse youngsters down on the Costa. Apart from the obvious pleasures of the beach or pool, which may suffice for some, the area has many other attractions aimed at entertaining young visitors. Aqua parks offer water slides, Kamikaze rapids and wave pools. Most close in winter, so check before you set out. Other attractions include the Sea Life Centre at Benalmádena's marina, the zoo at Fuengirola and the fun rides in mini-trains around some of the main resorts. Children will also enjoy the fun and colour of a local fiesta, should the opportunity arise.

BENALMÁDENA

SELWO MARINA

This marina/fauna park contains Andalucia's first dolphinarium and penguinarium. Exhibitions feature dolphins, sea lions and exotic birds. 3D cinemas and a children's playground offer plenty of fun all round.
D2 Parque de la Paloma, s/n, Benalmádena 902 19 04 82; www.selwomarina.com Daily 10–6 Expensive

TIVOLI WORLD, ARROYO DE LA MIEL

Amusement park including a giant rollercoaster, flamenco shows, a Wild West Town and live music. Tivolilandia is an infant area, and Tivoli Agua contains a water mountain flume ride.
D2 Avenida de Tivoli, s/n, Arroyo de la Miel 952 57 70 16; www.tivoliworld.com Apr, May, 15–30 Sep, Oct daily 4pm–1am; Jun, 1–14 Sep 5pm–2am; Jul, Aug 6pm–3am; Sat, Sun, Nov–Mar 1pm–10pm (times subject to change) Expensive (unlimited rides) Restaurants (€–€€) RENFE station Arroyo de la Miel Arroyo de la Miel Few

BENALMÁDENA COSTA

SEA LIFE BENALMÁDENA

Go on a voyage to the depths of the sea, with views of a wealth of marine life.
D2 Puerto Deportivo, Benalmádena 952 56 01 50; www.sealife.es Daily 10–6 Expensive Restaurant (€€) RENFE station Benalmádena Good

ESTEPONA

SELWO AVENTURA

A safari park where you can see animals from the five continents of the world, roaming around in a semi-wild habitat. Much of the tour is made by safari-style jeep.
B2 Autovía Costa del Sol, km 162.5, Las Lomas del Monte 902 19 04 82; www.selwo.es Jan–May, Oct–Dec, daily 10–6; Jun–Sep 10–7 Expensive Direct to Selwo (Costa line) Few

FUENGIROLA

ZOO FUENGIROLA

Modern zoo designed to re-create the natural habitiat of all the species living here. Wander among tropical forests, rivers and waterfalls to glimpse its varied flora and fauna, including chimpanzees, crocodiles, numerous birds and reptiles. Restaurants and a children's area.
D3 Camilio José Cela 6 952 66 63 01; www.zoofuengirola.com Daily 10–6 Expensive RENFE station Fuengirola

MARBELLA

FUNNY BEACH MARBELLA

Family leisure centre offering mostly water activities,

including water bikes, 'banana rides'. Also offers go-kart racing and quads.
C2 Ctra Cádiz 340, Marbella 952 82 33 59 Daily 11–11 Free

MIJAS COSTA

PARQUE ACUÁTICO MIJAS

This water theme park has great water chutes, including a thrilling Kamikaze, pools, slides and rapids.
Ctra N340, km 290 952 46 04 09; www.aquamijas.com May, daily 10–5.30; Jun, Sep 10–6; Jul, Aug 10–7; closed Oct–Apr Expensive Restaurant (€€) Fuengirola bus station Few

PUERTO BANÚS

SUPER BONANZA

The *Bonanza* departs every two hours from midday onwards for a cruise along the coast.
C2 Sinatra Bar, Puerto Banús 952 38 55 00

SENDA BIRD PARK

Wander around the tropical gardens and enjoy exotic birdlife. There's also an acquarium and reptile enclosure, as well as larger animals like giraffes.
C2 Ctra de Coín km 88, Churriana 952 62 35 40; www.sendaelretiro.com Daily 10–10 (to 6 in winter) Expensive Good

TORRE DEL MAR

PARQUE ACUÁTICO AQUAVELIS

Another fun water park with 12 different slides.
E2 Urb El Tomillar 952 54 25 92 Daily 10–6 Expensive Bus from Málaga (Torre del Mar stop) Few

TORREMOLINOS

AQUALAND

Water chutes, water mountains and artificial waves, plus mini park and restaurant.
D2 Ctra de Circunvalación (near Palacio de Congresos) 952 38 88 88; www.aqualand.es May–Sep daily 10–6 Expensive Restaurant (€€) Few

CROCODILE PARK

Centrally located, the park features more than 300 crocodiles, which can be viewed at close quarters. Guided visits with a crocodile trainer are available.
D2 Calle Cuba 14 952 05 17 82; www.crocodile-park.com Jul–Sep daily 10–7; Dec–Feb 10–5 Expensive RENFE Torremolinos Restaurant Few

CLUB EL RANCHITO

An impressive Andulusian horse spectacular.
D2 Senda del Pilar 4 952 38 30 63; www. ranchito.com Wed 5.45, Jun–Oct 6 Expensive Nearby Few

TAKE CARE

When taking children to southern Spain remember to take sensible precautions against over-exposure to the sun. It can be exceedingly hot during the summer months, so protective hats and high-factor sun blocks are strongly advised.

Places to Have Lunch

ALBAHACA (€)
A rare vegetarian restaurant on this carniverous Costa. The daily set menu is a real bargain.
✉ Doña Maria Barrabino 11, Torremolinos ☎ 952 37 51 82

CASA JUAN (€€)
Locals flock here to sample the legendary fresh seafood. There's outside seating on the pretty square.
✉ Plaza San Gines, La Carihuela ☎ 952 37 35 12

CASA PEDRO (€€)
One of the area's earliest restaurants. Seafood prepared Malaguenian style.
✉ Quitapeñas 121, Playa el Palo, Málaga ☎ 952 99 00 13

FRUTOS (€€€)
Known for superb Castilian cuisine including *jamón Ibérico*, suckling pig and lamb.
✉ Avenida Riviera 80, Los Alamos, Torremolinos ☎ 952 38 14 50

Enjoying a break in an outdoor café in Málaga

LA RADA (€–€€)
A lively atmosphere and quality fish and seafood dishes.
✉ Avenida de España, Estepona
☎ 952 79 10 36 🕒 Closed Tue

MESÓN CORDOBÉS (€€)
Excellent locaiton. Fish features on the menu with fresh catch of the day a good choice when available.
✉ Plaza de las Flores 15, Estepona
☎ 952 80 07 37

MESÓN EL COTO (€€)
Charcoal grilled lamb and suckling pig are specialities. In the mountains.
✉ Ctra San Pedro to Ronda (7km from San Pedro) ☎ 952 78 66 88

RESTAURANTE ANTONIO (€€–€€€)
One of the best restaurants overlooking the port. Speciality is sea bass baked in salt.
✉ Calle Muelle Rivera, Puerto Banús ☎ 952 81 35 36

EL ROQUEO (€€)
Good for fresh fish. Popular with locals.
✉ Carmen 35, La Carihuela, Torremolinos ☎ 952 38 49 46
🕒 Closed Tue and Nov

SANTIAGO (€€–€€€)
Considered to be one of Marbella's top restaurants.
✉ Paseo Marítimo, Marbella ☎ 952 77 0078

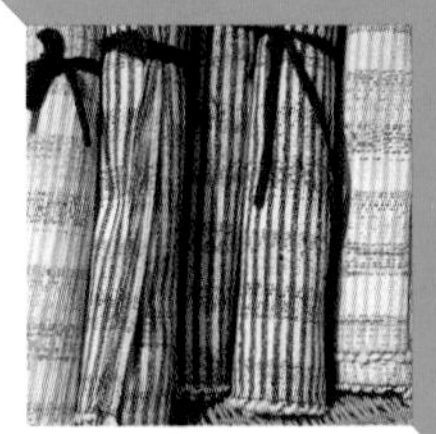

COSTA DEL SOL where to...

On the Costa del Sol & Beyond

PRICES

Prices are approximate, based on a three-course meal for one, including house wine, a beer or a soft drink and service:

€ = up to €18
€€ = €18–€35
€€€ = over €35

EATING COSTS

The cost of eating out along the coast varies widely. In the more fashionable restaurants prices can be on a par with top international restaurants anywhere. However, with careful selection, you can eat very well at reasonable cost.

Many restaurants offer a *menú del día* (menu of the day) that includes a two- or three-course meal and usually a drink as well. The price range varies according to the category of the restaurant and the area but you will usually get good value. In popular tourist centres, quality restaurants tend to serve only à la carte. While this may cost more the selection is greater, the quality of the food probably higher and you can still eat at affordable prices.

Some establishments also offer a *menú infantil* (children's menu), with smaller portions.

A *plato combinado* (combined plate), found in the more casual establishments, can fulfill the need for an adequate, low-cost meal.

ALMUÑECAR

JACQUY COTOBRO (€€)
A fine French restaurant at the foot of the Punta de la Mona. Cozy, with bare brick walls and green wicker chairs.
✉ Edificio Río, Playa Cotobro ☎ 958 63 18 02 🕑 Lunch and dinner

ANTEQUERA

CASERÍO SAN BENITO (€€)
Traditional eaterie north of Antequera with dishes, like *porra antequerana* (a thick version of gazpacho) and *migas* (fried bread crumbs with sausage).
✉ Ctra Málaga-Córdoba km 108 ☎ 952 11 11 03 🕑 Lunch and dinner

EL ANGELOTE (€€)
Atmospheric restaurant with two wood-beam dining rooms, Try the wild mushrooms in an almond and wine sauce.
✉ Plaza Cose Viejo ☎ 952 70 34 65 🕑 Lunch and dinner

ARROYO DE LA MIEL

VENTORILLO DE LA PERRA (€€€)
In an 18th-century inn. Cosy, attractive patio with plants. Spanish and international dishes.
✉ Avenida de la Constitución 85 ☎ 952 44 19 66 🕑 Lunch and dinner. Closed Mon

BENALMÁDENA COSTA

MAR DE ALBORÁN (€€)
Sophisticated restaurant with Basque-inspired seafood dishes located next to the port.
✉ Avenida de Alay 5 ☎ 952 44 64 27 🕑 Lunch and dinner

EL MERO (€€)
Top-quality restaurant. On the first-floor with views over the marina. Known for its fish, shellfish and barbecued meats.
✉ Dársena de Levante, Puerto Marina ☎ 952 44 07 52 🕑 Lunch and dinner

AIREN (€€€)
Creative international cuisine in elegant contemporary surroundings.
✉ Reserva del Higuerón ☎ 952 56 58 84 🕑 Tue–Sat lunch, Fri and Sat dinner

BENALMÁDENA PUEBLO

CASA FIDEL (€€)
Rustic atmosphere with large fireplace. International cuisine.
✉ Maestra Ayala 1 ☎ 952 44 91 65 🕑 Lunch and dinner. Closed Tue

CÓRDOBA

BANDELERO (€–€€)
Facing the Mezquita, this restaurant has an attractive bar and several dining rooms at the rear. Wide selection of tapas and simple dishes.
✉ Calle de Torrijos 6 ☎ 957 46 64 91 🕑 Lunch and dinner

EL CHURRASCO (€€)
Long-standing restaurant and lively tapas bar. Known for grilled meats.
✉ Romero 16 ☎ 957 29 08 17 🕑 Lunch and dinner. Closed Aug

ESTEPONA

BUENAVENTURA (€€€)
Top-quality restaurant offering creative cuisine. Outdoor dining in beautiful courtyard, where diners can watch operatic performances in August.
✉ Plaza de la Iglesia 5
☎ 952 85 80 69
🕓 Lunch and dinner. Closed Tue in winter and 15–30 Nov

EL CENACHERO (€€)
Located in the marina. Mediterranean cuisine, specialises in fresh shellfish, *zarzuelas*, fish baked in salt.
✉ Puerto Deportivo
☎ 952 80 14 42
🕓 Lunch and dinner. Closed Tue in winter and 15–30 Nov

FRIGILIANA

GARDEN RESTAURANT (€€)
Popular with foreign residents offering a casual atmosphere and wonderful views. Varied international menu.
✉ Calle Los Cubos ☎ 952 53 31 85 🕓 Lunch and dinner. Closed Tue

FUENGIROLA

LA LANGOSTA (€€)
Long-established favourite, renowned for its lobster dishes.
✉ Calle Francisco Cano 1, Los Bollichos ☎ 952 47 50 49
🕓 Dinner only. Closed Sun

PATRICK BAUSUER (€€€)
Excellent French restaurant with exquisite nouvelle-inspired dishes. There is complimentary champagne and hors d'oeuvres.
✉ Rotondade la Luna 1, Pueblo López ☎ 952 58 51 20
🕓 Dinner only

PORTOFINO (€€)
Italian specialities and international dishes in this restaurant on the seafront.
✉ Edificio Perla, Paseo Marítimo 29 ☎ 952 47 06 43 🕓 Lunch and dinner. Closed Mon, 1–15 Jul, 1–15 Dec. Dinner only in summer

LE VAGABOND (€)
Good value international cuisine with a friendly welcoming ambience. Attractive interior and a small terrace for outdoor dining in the summer.
✉ Calle de la Cruz 14 ☎ 952 46 21 46 🕓 Dinner only. Closed Wed

GRANADA

CHIKITO (€€)
Once frequented by writers and artists. Bar and restaurant known for its cured ham.
✉ Plaza del Campillo 9
☎ 958 22 33 64 🕓 Lunch and dinner. Closed Wed

MIRADOR DE MORAYMA (€€€)
Fine views of the Alhambra. Country-style décor, lively ambience.
✉ Pianista Gracia Carillo 2
☎ 952 22 82 90
🕓 Lunch and dinner. Closed Sun

SEVILLA (€€)
Old haunt of García Lorca and Manuel de Falla. Attractive dining rooms, open terrace.
✉ Oficios 12 ☎ 958 22 12 23
🕓 Lunch and dinner. Closed Sun

TAPAS

Tapas bars are a way of life in Spain and a visit to some of these establishments in the old part of Málaga will give a feel of the town. A lively atmosphere is usually provided by local people, who meet regularly for animated conversation over a beer or a chilled *fino* sherry. The choice of tapas can range from olives, almonds and *jamón serrano* (cured ham) to *tortilla* slices (Spanish-style omelette), vegetable dishes and a selection of fish and seafood, often well laced with garlic.

Porciones denote smaller helpings, while *raciones* are more ample. The bars are open for most of the day to serve drinks and food.

BUDGET FOOD

For inexpensive eating and an informal atmosphere, the coast offers a variety of options. In addition to the famous tapas bars, there are *bodegas*, *tabernas* and *cervecerías*, all of which are basically bars that serve food as well. Then there are the popular *chiringuitos*, casual open-air beach bars/restaurants, found along the length of the coast. A *marisquería* is a restaurant that specialises in seafood, while an *asado* offers barbecued food, usually meats.

MÁLAGA

ACEITE Y PAN (€€)
Select the fish you fancy from the tank and eat the same exquisitely prepared at a streetside table.
✉ Calle Cervantes 5 ☎ 952 60 94 22 🕐 Lunch and dinner

ADOLFO (€€)
Known for excellent local and international cuisine.
✉ Paseo Marítimo Pablo Ruiz Picasso 12 ☎ 952 60 19 14 🕐 Lunch and dinner. Closed Sun

LE ALEGRIA (€€)
A traditional restaurant with terracotta tiles, tapas bar and menu of local malagueño dishes.
✉ Calle Marin Garcia 15 ☎ 952 21 52 52 🕐 Lunch and dinner. Closed Sun

ANTONIO MARTÍN (€€€)
Seafront restaurant with large terrace; specialising in seafood.
✉ Paseo Marítimo ☎ 952 22 73 98 🕐 Lunch and dinner. Closed Sun dinner

CAFÉ CENTRAL (€)
Tables spill out onto the pretty historic square at this all-day dining spot.
✉ Plaza de la Constitución 11 ☎ 952 22 49 72 🕐 All day

CAFÉ DE PARÍS (€€€)
Elegant restaurant known for its quality of food and service.
✉ Calle Vélez Málaga ☎ 952 22 50 43 🕐 Lunch and dinner. Closed Mon, dinner Sun

LA CANCELA (€)
Specialities include *fritura malagueña* and *ajo blanco* (cold garlic and almond soup).
✉ Calle Denis Belgrano 3 ☎ 952 22 31 25 🕐 Lunch and dinner. Closed Wed evening

CASA DEL GUARDIA
Dating from 1840, this is Málaga's oldest bars. A good place for sweet wines and fresh prawns.
✉ Alameda Principal ☎ None 🕐 Lunch and dinner

EL CHINITAS (€€)
Lively, known for its tapas. Specialises in Andalusian and Mediterranean dishes.
✉ Calle Moreno Monroy 4–6 ☎ 952 21 09 72 🕐 Lunch and dinner

EL LEGADO CELESTIAL (€)
Chinese restaurant with an excellent-value daily buffet.
✉ Calle Medelin 3 ☎ 952 35 25 21 🕐 Lunch and dinner. Closed Sun

EL VEGETARIANO DE LA ALCAZABILLA (€)
Reliably good vegetarian restaurant with a very reasonable daily menu, plus extensive à la carte choice.
✉ Pozo del Rey 5 ☎ 952 21 48 58 🕐 Lunch and dinner. Closed Sun

LO GÜENO (€)
Typical tapas bar. Known for its excellent ham.
✉ Calle Marín García 9 ☎ 952 22 21 80 🕐 Lunch and dinner

MESÓN ASTORGA (€€)
Traditional Andalusían cuisine.
✉ Calle Gerona 11 ☎ 952 34 25 63 🕐 Lunch and dinner. Closed Wed

MARBELLA

CALIFORNIA (€)
Casual ambience, popular with the locals. Good value fish and seafood tapas.
✉ Calle Málaga 2, Edif, So. No. 2 ☎ 952 86 67 52 ⏲ Lunch and dinner. Closed Sun

GOIZEKO AND DALLI'S (€€€)
Basque and Italian cuisine complemented with superb service in fabulous surroundings.
✉ Urb. Mansion Club ☎ 952 76 90 30 ⏲ Lunch and dinner

LA HACIENDA (€€€)
Top restaurant with a reputation for *haute cuisine*. Sea views.
✉ Urbanización Las Chapas, N340 (12km east of Marbella) ☎ 952 83 11 16 ⏲ Dinner only in summer. Closed Mon, Tue and mid-Nov to mid-Dec

LA PESQUERA (€)
Bar and restaurant serving good seafood.
✉ Plaza de la Victoria s/n ☎ 952 77 80 54 ⏲ Lunch and dinner

LA PESQUERA DEL FARO (€€)
Well-positioned, overlooking the sea, this has the atmosphere of a beach hotel. Good food: specialities include fish baked in salt and seafood dishes. Steps lead down to a terrace right on the beach below, adjoining Marbella's marina
✉ Playa del Faro, Paseo del Marítimo ☎ 952 8685 20 ⏲ Lunch and dinner

ZOZOI (€€€)
Creative cuisine with fusion starters like Thai fish cakes with fresh arugula salad, plus more than 45 different vodkas, as well as some unusual wines and liquors.
✉ Plaza Altamirano 1 ☎ 952 85 88 68 ⏲ Dinner only

MIJAS

BAR PORRAS (€€€)
At the base of the most photographed street in the village attracts a regular crowd of crusty locals with its good-value tasty tapas. Outside seating in the summer.
✉ Plaza de la Libertad ☎ None ⏲ All day

EL MIRLO BLANCO (€€)
Basque and international cuisine. Outdoor terrace overlooking the charming little square of Plaza de la Constitución.
✉ Plaza Constitución 2 ☎ 952 48 57 00 ⏲ Lunch and dinner

EL PADTRASTO (€€€)
Spectacular clifftop location. Terrace with views of Fuengirola and the coast. Top-class local and international cooking. Access by lift or a steep flight of stairs.
✉ Paseo del Compás 22 ☎ 952 48 50 00 ⏲ Lunch and dinner

VALPARAÍSO (€€)
In an attractive villa with a terrace, gardens and a pool, this is ideal for a dinner-dancing evening.
✉ Carretera de Fuengirola, km 4 ☎ 952 48 59 96 ⏲ Dinner only. Closed Sun in winter

WHAT TO DRINK

Wine is widely drunk with meals, with a preference for red wine, sometimes taken chilled. White and rosé wines are also available and a pleasant alternative is a jug of *sangría*. Based on a combination of red wine, fruit and a liqueur, topped up with lemonade and ice, this is best enjoyed when eating in the open air on a sunny day.

Spain has excellent beer, fruit juices and soft drinks. An acquired taste is *Horchata*, a non-alcoholic drink based on almonds and barley.

To round off your meal, there is a wide range of *coñacs* (Spanish brandy) ranging from the inexpensive Fundador or Terry, to the special savour of a Carlos I.

HEALTHY INGREDIENTS

Olives have been cultivated since the time of the Greeks and Andalucía produces one of the most important olive crops in the world. The production of olive oil involves arduous work, from the collection of the crops towards December to the first pressing, which is known as virgin oil.

Olive oil forms an integral part of Spanish cooking and scientific research suggests it is good for the health, as is garlic, which also features widely in Spanish cuisine.

EAT SPANISH

Restaurants along the coast tend to specialise in fish and seafood. Top-class grilled meats and international cuisine are also much in evidence, however, with all tastes catered for. Local Andalusian cooking is more likely to be found in smaller restaurants or away from the coast and tourist areas. Here you will find an emphasis on tasty homemade soups, vegetables prepared in a variety of ways, meat and game dishes, often served as a stew.

In line with much of the country, the Andalusians tend to eat late: lunch is normally taken from about 2pm and can well carry on to early evening!

Many diners will arrive around 10pm or so. The trendier the place, the later the action. Many restaurants are closed one day a week. This varies from one restaurant to another, so check if in doubt. Some may open for dinner only. Note also that some restaurants may close for a while in summer and/or during holiday periods in winter.

NERJA

PEPE RICO (€€€)
Housed in a mansion, where top-class meals are served in the elegant dining room or on the flower-filled patio.
✉ Almirante Ferrándiz 28
☎ 952 52 02 47
🕒 Lunch and dinner. Closed Tue, 1–15 Dec, 15 Jan–15 Feb, Sun

SCARLETT'S (€€)
Trendy restaurant with innovative menu and stylish interior. There are two outside terraces. The menu includes a delicious *gambas pil-pil* (prawns fried in garlic).
✉ Calle Cristo 38 ☎ 952 52 00 11 🕒 Lunch and dinner

NUEVA ANDALUCÍA

DIVINA GULA (€€)
International cuisine. Specialities include Argentinian-style grilled meats, fresh pasta dishes, lamb and fish.
✉ Plaza la Orquídea s/n, Nueva Andalucía (opposite Puerto Banús) ☎ 952 81 87 00
🕒 Lunch and dinner

PUERTO BANÚS

AZUL MARINO (€€)
Brasserie-restaurant, good for fish and seafood.
✉ Front Line, Port I
☎ 952 81 10 44
🕒 Lunch and dinner

LA CARACOLA DEL PUERTO (€€)
Known for its paellas and tapas. In a good spot overlooking the quay.
✉ Muelle Benabola 5
☎ 952 81 16 84
🕒 Lunch and dinner. Closed Tue

CHRISTIAN (€€)
One of Puerto Banús' first restaurants, is still popular.
✉ In the port ☎ 952 81 10 06 🕒 Lunch and dinner

DON LEONE (€€€)
Long-time favourite, open-air, overlooking marina. Italian cuisine.
✉ Muelle Ribera ☎ 952 81 17 16 🕒 Lunch and dinner

EGAN'S BAR RESTAURANT (€€)
Home-cooked fresh food with a creative flair, from tapas to a full à la carte menu.
✉ Avenida Los Girasoles
☎ 952 81 46 73 🕒 Lunch and dinner

SALOBREÑA

EL PEÑON (€€)
Stunning spot on the rocks with a good menu of mostly seafood dishes.
✉ Paseo Martimo s/n ☎ 958 61 05 38 🕒 Lunch and dinner

SAN PEDRO DE ALCÁNTARA

AMICI (€)
Adventurous and creative dishes made with all fresh ingredients. An excellent spot for breakfast as well.
✉ Centro la Colonia
☎ 952 85 35 74
🕒 Breakfast, lunch and dinner

GAMBASOL (€)
Family-run restaurant specialising in English and Scandinavian dishes.
✉ Urb. las Petunias ☎ 952 77 82 12 🕒 Lunch and dinner

VICTOR (€€)
Specialities include rack of lamb and sea bass.

✉ Centro Comercial Guadalmina, local 1 ☎ 952 88 34 91 ⌚ Lunch and dinner. Closed Sun dinner and Mon

SAN ROQUE

LOS REMOS (€€€)
High-class restaurant in a neoclassical villa with attractive gardens. Good for fish and seafood.
✉ Villa Victoria S, Campamento
☎ 956 69 84 12
⌚ Lunch and dinner. Closed Sun

SEVILLA

LA ALBAHACA (€€)
In a typical Andalusían house, decorated with tiles and plants. French and Spanish cuisine.
✉ Plaza Santa Cruz
☎ 954 22 07 14
⌚ Lunch and dinner. Closed Sun

CASA ROBLES (€€)
Traditional restaurant near the cathedral. Classic Andalusian dishes and a lively tapas bar downstairs.
✉ Calle Álvarez Quinters 58
☎ 954 56 32 72
⌚ Lunch and dinner

EL GIRALDILLO (€€)
Facing the cathedral and La Giralda. Tables out on the pavement for a casual drink and a light meal.
✉ Plaza Virgen de los Reyes 2
☎ 954 21 45 25
⌚ Lunch and dinner

TABERNA DEL ALABARDERO (€€€)
Delightful restaurant in a 19th-century villa dishing up modern dishes like grilled cod with mushrooms in a spicy chilli and ham sauce. Fronted by a bar and terrace for al fresco dining.
✉ Zaragoza 20 ☎ 954 56 06 37 ⌚ Lunch and dinner

TORREMOLINOS

LA BODEGA (€)
Constantly busy with locals and tourists.
✉ Calle San Miguel 40
☎ 952 38 73 37
⌚ Lunch and dinner

BODEGAS QUITAPEÑAS (€)
Reliably excellent traditional bodega serving seafood tapas and ice cold fino straight from the barrel.
✉ Cuesta del Tajo 3 ☎ 952 38 62 44 ⌚ All day

LA CHACHA (€)
This open-air seafood tapas bar is an institution.
✉ Palma de Mallorca 3
☎ None ⌚ Lunch and dinner

LA JÁBEGA (€€)
This lively restaurant along the promenade serves a good choice of meat, fish and seafood.
✉ Calle Mar 15, La Carihuela
☎ 952 38 63 75
⌚ Lunch and dinner

LA MANCHA (€€)
Traditional Spanish game dishes.
✉ Avenida Los Manatiales, Plaza Goya ☎ 952 38 01 46
⌚ Lunch and dinner

RESTAURANTE ANTONIO (€€€)
Well positioned on the promenade. International menu.
✉ Plaza del Remo s/n, La Carihuela ☎ 952 05 07 35
⌚ Lunch and dinner

LOCAL DELICACIES

A popular starter is the Andalusian speciality *gazpacho Andaluz*, a chilled tomato soup with additions, although this is not always on the menu in winter. Other favourites are asparagus, *jamón serrano* (cured ham), *entremés de carne* (cold meats), tuna salad and *calamares a la romana* (fried squid rings).

For the main course there is often a good selection of fish dishes, although they can be pricey. *Fritura Malagueña* (an assortment of fried fish) and fish baked in salt are specialities, while you can always ask for the catch of the day. Otherwise pork, chicken and rabbit, grilled (*a la plancha*) or prepared with a sauce, are usually a good bet. There is always paella, which can be taken as a first or main course.

Desserts tend to be limited, with *flan* (crème caramel), ice-cream or fresh fruit of the season among the most popular choices.

On the Costa del Sol & Beyond

PRICES

Prices are approximate, for a double room, including breakfast and IVA (VAT):

€ = under €60
€€ = €60–€150
€€€= over €150

HOTEL GRADINGS

Officially registered hotels range from 1 to 5 star (with an additional top deluxe category of GL, Gran Lujo). Other types of accommodation include apartment hotels, hotel *residencias* (no restaurant), hostels and pensions. Stars are assigned according to services and facilities available. Suites can usually be found in the 4 or 5-star range. Tariffs should be displayed in the lobby.

ALMUÑECAR

CASABLANCA (€)
Moorish-style hotel with spacious rooms and views over the sea or the castle and mountains behind.
✉ Plaza San Cristóbal 4
☎ 958 6355 59

ANTEQUERA

PARADOR DE ANTEQUERA (€)
Modern building set attractively among ruins of the Moorish fortress.
✉ García de Olmo s/n ☎ 952 84 02 61; www.parador.es

BENALMÁDENA COSTA

BALI HOTEL (€€)
Popular family hotel close to restaurants, the port and the nightlife.
✉ Avenida de Telefonica 7
☎ 952 44 19 40

TRITON (€€)
Established in subtropical gardens, with mountain and sea views. Pools and floodlit tennis courts.
✉ Avenida Antonio Machado 29
☎ 952 44 32 40;
www.besthotels.es

CÓRDOBA

AMISTAD CÓRDOBA (€€€)
Two 18th-century mansions stylishly converted, with mudéjar courtyard, carved-wood ceiling and plush rooms.
✉ Place de Maimónides 3
☎ 957 42 03 35; www.nh-hoteles.com

MEZQUITA (€€)
In a 16th-century house. Attractive décor, opposite the Mosque.
✉ Plaza Santa Cataline 1
☎ 957 47 55 85

ESTEPONA

ALBERO LODGE (€€)
Boutique hotel with each room named after a city with décor to match. Private terraces and direct access to beach.
✉ Urb. Finca La Cancelada, Calle Tamesis 16 ☎ 952 88 07 00; www.alberolodge.com

ATALAYA PARK (€€€)
In lovely gardens, facing the beach. Extensive sports facilities.
✉ Carretera N340 ☎ 952 88 90 00; www.atalaya-park.es

LAS DUNAS BEACH HOTEL & SPA (€€€)
On the beach, between Marbella and Estepona. Tropical gardens, Andalusían-style décor. Pool, gourmet restaurant, watersports, riding and beauty clinic.
✉ La Boladilla Baja, Ctra de Cádiz, km 163.5 ☎ 952 79 43 45; www.las-dunas.com

EL PARAÍSO (€€€)
On a hill with good views of the coast and attractive gardens, surrounded by a golf course. Large outdoor and heated pool, riding. Chinese medical centre.
✉ Ctra de Cádiz, km 134
☎ 952 88 30 00;
www.hotelparaisocoastadelsol.com

FUENGIROLA

HOSTAL ITALIA (€)
In the centre of town. Warm family atmosphere, good value.

✉ Calle de la Cruz 1
☏ 952 47 41 93

HOSTAL MARBELLA (€)
Swedish owned small hostal with pleasant rooms near the beach.
✉ Calle Marbella 34
☏ 952 66 45 03; www.hostalmarbella.info

HOTEL PUERTO (€€)
Right on the beach with spacious bright rooms and a rooftop swimming pool.
✉ Paseo Marítimo 32
☏ 952 47 01 00; www.hotel-elpuerto.com

LAS PIRÁMIDES (€€)
On the Paseo Marítimo, near the beach and the town centre. A garden and pool, flamenco shows and live music. Golf, mini-golf and tennis nearby.
✉ Miquel Márquez, 43
☏ 952 47 06 00

VILLA DE LAREDO (€€)
Pleasant medium-sized hotel on the promenade.
✉ Paseo Marítimo 42
☏ 952 47 76 89; www.hotelvilladelaredo.com

GRANADA

ALHAMBRA PALACE (€€)
Traditional favourite with Moorish-style décor. Near the Alhambra. Views of the Sierra Nevada from some rooms.
✉ Calle Peña Partida, 2
☏ 958 22 14 68; www.h-alhambrapalace.es

NH INGLATERRA (€€)
Pleasant, central hotel, in a 19th-century house.
✉ Cetti Meriem 4 ☏ 958 22 15 59; www.nh-hotels.com

MÁLAGA

DON CURRO (€€)
Medium-range hotel, conveniently positioned between the old town and the seafront.
✉ Sancha de Lara 7
☏ 952 22 72 00; www.doncurro.com

HOTEL ATARAZANAS (€€)
New hotel just across from the central market in an elegant building. Rooms are small but comfortable and modern. Café and excellent restaurant.
✉ Calle Atarazanas 19
☏ 952 12 19 10; www.balboahoteles.com

PARADOR MÁLAGA-GIBRALFARO (€€)
Attractively situated high up the hill by Gibralfaro Castle with magnificent views of Málaga and the bay.
✉ Gibralfaro ☏ 952 22 19 02; www.parador.es

MARBELLA

ANDALUCÍA PLAZA (€€)
Spacious. Atractive décor; garden, pools, sports facilities, casino.
✉ Nueva Andalucía
☏ 952 81 20 00; www.hotelandaluciaplaza.com

ARTOLA (€€)
Pretty hotel decorated with yellow trim and green shutters. Rooms have balconies and there is a 9-hole golf course, plus pool and nearby beach.
✉ Ctra. de Cádiz, km 194
☏ 952 93 13 90; www.hotelartola.com

TRAVELLERS WITH DISABILITIES

Facilities for travellers with disabilities are slowly improving in Andalucía. Gradually more hotels are offering fixed and mobile ramps, special lifts, wider doorways, corridors and toilets to accommodate wheelchairs and designated parking areas close to the hotel entrance. If such services are required, check they are available at the hotel before booking.

For further information on facilities for visitors with disabilities contact the following organisations:
Independent Living Spain, Mijas Costa
☏ 952 49 34 19, www.independentlivingspain.com
Lux Mundi, Fuengirola
☏ 952 47 48 40
Mobility Abroad, Benalmadena
☏ 952 44 77 64, www.mobilityabroad. com (also rents Mobility Scooters).

PARADORES

Very pleasant accommodation is provided by the *parador*, originally denoting a lodging place for the gentry. The late 1920s saw the development of this network of state-run establishments. Often in attractively converted old castles and historic buildings, *paradores* are scattered throughout the country, making good stop-overs when touring by car. There are also some purpose-built modern *paradores* in tourist centres, many set in tranquil gardens, often with a pool, in lovely surroundings. Although tariffs have risen over the years, the splendour of the buildings and their locations make an overnight stay worthwhile.

EL FUERTE (€€)
Attractive hotel in pleasant gardens. Near the sea and within walking distance of Marbella centre.
✉ Avenida El Fuerte
☎ 952 86 15 00;
www.fuertehotels.com

HOTEL FUERTE MIRAMAR-SPA (€€€)
Modern El Fuerte group hotel on the seafront offering outdoor heated pool, a hydrotherapy centre and good facilities.
✉ Plaza José Luque Manzano, s/n ☎ 952 76 84 10;
www.fuertehoteles.com

LIMA (€€)
Medium-range hotel; close to the old town and a short walk to the seafront.
✉ Avenida Antonio Belón
☎ 952 77 05 00

MARBELLA CLUB (€€)
Luxurious old time favourite, set in lush gardens with swimming pool, restaurants, beach bar and boutiques.
✉ Blvd Príncipe Alfonso de Hohenlohe ☎ 952 82 22 11;
www.marbellaclub.com

PUENTE ROMANO (€€€)
Super deluxe village-like complex with landscaped gardens, pool, tennis.
✉ Carretera N340, between Marbella and Puerto Banús
☎ 952 82 09 00;
www.puenteromano.com

RUI RINCÓN ANDALUZ (€€)
Attractive complex built in an Andalusian-style pueblo. Near the sea.
✉ N349 km 173 ☎ 952 81 15 17; www.riu.com

SAN CRISTÓBAL (€)
Modest, and convenient for Marbella centre.
✉ Ramon y Cajal 3
☎ 952 77 12 50

MIJAS

HOTEL MIJAS (€)
At the entrance to Mijas, with superb views down to the coast. Pool.
✉ Urb Tamisa s/n ☎ 952 48 58 00

MONDA

CASTILLO DE MONDA (€€)
Old castle converted into a hotel. Moorish-style furnishings and views of the Sierra de las Nieves.
✉ Monda (18km northeast of Marbella) ☎ 952 45 71 42;
www.mondacastle.com

NERJA

BALCÓN DE EUROPA (€€)
Old favourite on the promenade. Private beach.
✉ Paseo Balcón de Europa
☎ 952 52 08 00;
www.balcondeeuropa.com

HOTEL CARABEO (€€)
Tucked away down a side street, this boutique hotel has rooms with sea views, plus a small gym and games room.
✉ Calle Hernando de Carabeo 34 ☎ 952 52 54 44;
www.hotelcarabeo.com

PARADOR DE NERJA (€€)
Modern *parador* set high up with pleasant gardens. Splendid views of the bay.
✉ Almuñécar 8 ☎ 952 52 00 50; www.parador.es

RONDA

ANCINIPO (€€)
The artistic legacy of former owners and local artists is in evidence throughout this boutique hotel. The creative, interior has exposed stone panels, steel-and-glass fittings, and mosaic-tile bathrooms.
✉ José Aparicio 7 ☎ 952 16 10 02; www.hotelacinipo.com

REINA VICTORIA (€€)
An old favourite, built in the early 20th century. Gardens, pool and views.
✉ Calle Jerez 25 ☎ 952 87 12 40; hotelreinavictoria.com

SAN GABRIEL (€€)
Delightful hotel with tasteful décor, in an 18th-century mansion with attractive courtyard.
✉ Marqués de Moctezuma 19
☎ 952 19 03 92;
www.hotelsangabriel.com

SAN PEDRO DE ALCÁNTARA

PUEBLO ANDALUZ (€€)
Typical Andalusian-style establishment. Pool, tennis and gardens.
✉ Avenida Luis Carilllo Benítez
☎ 952 78 05 97

SEVILLA

ALFONSO XIII (€€€)
One of Spain's most famous hotels. Built around a large courtyard with arches and greenery. Marble floors, panelled ceilings and ceramic tiles. Gardens and pool.
✉ Calle San Fernando 2
☎ 954 91 70 00;
www.westin.com/hotelalfonso

BÉCQUER (€€)
Pleasant hotel near the town centre and the river.
✉ Calle Reyes Católicos 4
☎ 954 22 89 00;
www.hotelbecquer.com

HOSTERÍA DEL LAUREL (€€)
In the heart of the Barrio de Santa Cruz. Restaurant in a pretty square.
✉ Plaza de los Venerables 5
☎ 954 22 02 95;
www.hosteriadellaurel.com

HOTEL AMADEUS (€€)
Small hotel of great charm that will appeal to music lovers. Family run.
✉ Calle Farnesio 6
☎ 954 50 14 43;
www.hotelamadeussevilla.com

TORREMOLINOS

CERVANTES (€€)
Large, modern hotel close the centre. Garden, two pools, restaurants, live music and dancing.
✉ Calle Las Mercedes s/n
☎ 952 38 40 33; www.hotelcervantestorremolinos.es

MIAMI (€)
Something of a find, this small hotel built in 1950 was designed by Manolo Blascos, Picasso's cousin. Surrounded by a shady garden, its like staying at a private Spanish home.
✉ Aladino 14 ☎ 952 38 52 55; www.residencia-miami.com

TROPICANA HOTEL AND BEACH CLUB (€€€)
Colourful tropical look; kidney-shape pool in the gardens and a beach club.
✉ Calle Trópico 6, La Carihuela
☎ 952 38 66 00; www.hotel-tropicana.net

RURAL RETREATS

As a total contrast to the beach, visitors may like to venture into Andalucía's hinterland. A number of so-called rural lodgings can be found a short distance from the coast, which can vary from country cottages and rooms in attractive *haciendas* to mountain refuges or hostels and facilities for camping. In addition to wonderful scenery and fresh mountain air, there are often possibilities for hiking, riding and other pursuits.

Information and reservation centre:
RAAR (Red Andaluza de Alojamientos Rurales)
✉ Apdo 2035, 04080 Almería
☎ 902 44 22 33;
fax: 950 27 16 78; www.raar.es

You can also contact:
AHRA (Asocación de Hoteles Rurales de Andalucía)
✉ Calle Ramal Hoyo, Torremolinos ☎ 952 37 87 75, www.ahra.es
Rustic Blue ✉ Barrio La Ermita, Bubión, Granada
☎ 952 76 33 81;
www.rusticblue.com
Casa Andaluza ☎ 956 45 60 53; www.-andaluza.com
Rural Andalus
✉ Calle Don Cristián 10, 29007 Málaga
☎ 952 27 62 29;
fax: 952 27 65 567;
www.ruralandalus.es

Fashion & Jewellery

SHOPPING IN MÁLAGA

The most concentrated shopping area in Málaga is in and around Calle Marqués de Larios, north of the Alameda Principal, Málaga's main boulevard. Within easy walking distance are a host of shops and boutiques that stock a variety of goods, geared more to local needs than to visiting tourists. If you take time to browse around, however, you will come across some very attractive ceramics and handicrafts, antiques, leather goods (shoes can be a good buy) and jewellery, in addition to the odd souvenir and gift shop.

FUENGIROLA

CAPUCINE
Top names in fashion, including Versace, Naf-Naf, Guess and Monari.
✉ Miramar-Fuengirola
☎ 952 19 83 87

NICHOLSON
Modern jewellery designs. Just off Orange Square.
✉ Calle Marbella s/n
☎ 952 47 58 82

MÁLAGA

BLANCO
Funky and fashionable street and party wear for teens.
✉ Centro Comercial Larios
☎ 952 36 93 17

MANGO
A branch of Spain's well-known chain of elegant fashion stores.
✉ Larios 1 ☎ 952 22 31 02

MARBELLA

DON MIGUEL
Long established, with wide range of fashionwear for men and women.
✉ Avenida Ricardo Soriano 5
☎ 952 77 31 40

GUCCI
No introduction needed.
✉ Calle Valdéz 8
☎ 952 86 14 99

JOYERIA TIRADO
Beautiful handcrafted jewellery.
✉ Tetuán 12 ☎ 952 77 50 40

LOUIS FERAUD
Striking designs and vibrant colours.
✉ Plaza Victoria
☎ 952 82 81 06

NERJA

BRUNA CAVVALINI
Clothes from Sevilla and London. Look for bargains.
✉ Calle Barrio ☎ 952 52 30 58

MAVI
Jewellery and watches.
✉ Avenida Castilla Perez
☎ 952 53 86 26

PUERTO BANÚS

BOUTIQUE DONNA PIU
Italian-style fashion.
✉ Paseo Benabola L87
☎ 952 81 49 90

BOUTIQUE NUMBER ONE
French and Italian designer collections.
✉ Levante 1 ☎ 952 81 16 97

GIANNI VERSACE
For the fashion conscious.
✉ Centro Comercial Benabola 8
☎ 952 81 02 96

SAN PEDRO DE ALCÁNTARA

ANTHONY'S JEWELLERS
Unusual and original designs by the owner.
✉ Plaza las Faroles
☎ 952 78 62 74

TORRE DEL MAR

SINGH
Top fashion names.
✉ Calle Avenida de Andalucía 121 ☎ 952 54 10 91

TORREMOLINOS

DON LAL
Silver, crystal and Lladró, plus fine jewellery.
✉ Calle San Miguel 50
☎ 952 38 61 15

Antiques, Books & Ceramics

ANTIQUE SHOPS

GRANADA

GONZÁLO REYES MUÑOZ
✉ Calle Mesones (Placeta de Cauchiles 1) ☎ 958 52 32 74

MÁLAGA

REDING 41
✉ Paseo de Reding 41
☎ 952 22 96 60

EL TRIANON
✉ Madre de Dios 22
☎ 952 21 08 46

MARBELLA

EL RASTRO
Dates from 1955 with a selection of old paintings, furniture, sculptures and smaller items.
✉ Ctra Cádiz, km 176
☎ 952 82 23 44

RONDA

MUÑOZ SOTO
✉ B S Juan de Dios de Córdoba 34 ☎ 952 87 14 51

SAN PEDRO DE ALCÁNTARA

EL TERRAL
Mostly dark wood and rustic Andalusian furniture.
✉ La Concho 1
☎ 952 78 88 08

BOOKS

NERJA

NERJA BOOK CENTRE
Large secondhand bookshop.
✉ Calle Granda 30
☎ 952 52 09 08

CERAMICS

ESTEPONA

CERÁMICA LA CHIMINEA
Beautiful designs created by Paco Leonicio, who learnt his crafts at Triana, one of Spain's top centres for pottery. Wide selection of hand-painted tiles, glazed and unglazed ceramics.
✉ Calle El Cerrillo 6 ☎ 952 79 44 75

MÁLAGA

CERÁMICA FINA
Cerámica Fina stocks attractively displayed ceramics of all kinds showing a high standard of workmanship.
✉ Calle Coronel 5, near the church of San Juan
☎ 952 22 46 06

SEVILLA

SEVILLARTE
A wide range of beautiful ceramic products at three different branches.
✉ Gloria 5 ☎ 954 21 88 35;
✉ Sierpes 66
☎ 954 21 28 36;
✉ Vida 13 ☎ 954 56 29 45

CERÁMICA SANTA ISABEL
A typical ceramic shop and warehouse in the atmospheric barrio of Triana.
✉ Alfareria 12
☎ 954 34 46 08

MARTIAN CERAMICS
High-quality decorative plates and ceramics.
✉ Sierpes 74
☎ 954 21 34 13

PUERTO BANÚS

Puerto Banús is a very different shopping scene. Former orange-growing farmlands were developed in the 1960s by the businessman Don José Banús to become the successful international centre it is today.

For those who like to shop at trendy boutiques stocked with designer goods, against the glamorous background of yachts and a chic ambience, Puerto Banús is a veritable mecca – at a price!

Leatherware & Gifts

MARKETS

Street markets in Spain are great fun to visit. Major centres along the coast have a weekly market, generally open from early in the morning to around 2.30pm.

Fruit and vegetable displays create a profusion of colour. In addition to enjoying the lively ambience of clamour and bustling activity, there is always the chance of picking up a bargain. Popular items for bringing back as gifts include pottery and ceramics, leatherware, straw baskets, hats and the occasional piece of costume jewellery.

LEATHERWARE

BENALMÁDENA

ARTESANÍA PIEL
Leather goods produced on the premises. Out-of-the-ordinary belts.
✉ Puerto Marina ☎ None

FUENGIROLA

BRAVO
Good reputation for shoes, handbags and luggage. Also has shops in Marbella and Torremolinos.
✉ Avenida Condes de San Isidro 33 ☎ 952 46 17 19

MÁLAGA

NARTÍN SÁENZ
Top quality leather suitcases, bags, gloves and briefcases.
✉ Calle Larios 2
☎ 952 21 47 85

ROSSELLI
Leather shoes and bags, for women and men.
✉ Calle Molino Larios
☎ 952 21 43 23

MARBELLA

CHARLES JOURDAN
Wide range of shoes and leather goods. Other items include jewellery, umbrellas and sunglasses.
✉ Avenida Ramón y Cajal
☎ 952 77 00 03

TORREMOLINOS

BAZAR CANADÁ
This leather specialist is a good place to go for handbags, coats and clothing.
✉ Calle Peligro 11, El Bajondillo
☎ 952 37 28 29

GIFT SHOPS

BENALMÁDENA

MAISON EN FLEUR
Artwork and gift items for the home.
✉ Puerto Marina
☎ 952 57 61 72

FUENGIROLA

REGALOS DE ARTE MAXI
Lladró porcelain, ceramics from Sevilla, Majorcan pearls and other gifts.
✉ Avenida Ramón y Cajal 1
☎ 952 47 33 34

MÁLAGA

ETCETERA
Fun fashionable shop with plenty of gift ideas.
✉ Calle Echegaray 2
☎ 952 22 60 05

MARBELLA

REGALOS INMACULADA
Lots of gifts, including ceramics, jewellery and textiles.
✉ Pedraza 4 ☎ 952 77 13 26

TORREMOLINOS

PLAYASOL
One of a strip of souvenir shops, but better than most – and cheaper.
✉ Calle Carihuela 38
☎ 952 38 74 40

REGALOS GENI
Wide range of gifts, including good selection of Lladró, Swarovski crystal and Joseph Bofill sculpture.
✉ Calle San Miguel 8
☎ 952 38 28 05

Food, Wine & Stores

FOOD AND WINE

PUERTO BANÚS

SEMON
Quality deli selling a wide range of items, including national and imported cheeses, caviar,, smoked salmon and cold meats. There's also a small bar here for salads, healthy sandwiches and drinks.
✉ Gregorio Marañon s/n
☎ 952 77 77 96

SAN PEDRO ALCÁNTARA

ANDRÉS INGELMO MARCOS
Quality Iberian ham and sausages, also cheeses from Zamora and Valladolid and Rioja wines.
✉ Calle Miguel Hernández 4
☎ 952 78 65 56

STORES

FUENGIROLA

CENTRO COMERICAL PARQUE MARAMAR
Opened in 2005, this commercial centre covers some 45,000sq m and has more than 100 boutiques, restaurants, cinemas, supermarket and more.
✉ Parque Miramar
☎ 952 19 84 27

MÁLAGA

EL CORTE INGLÉS
This chain has many stores throughout the area; this one has six floors of fashion, gifts, exhibitions of arts and crafts.
✉ Avenida de Andalucia 4–6
☎ 952 30 00 00

LARIOS CENTRE
Over 125 shops, restaurants and cinema complex; three hours free parking.
✉ Avenida de la Aurora 25
☎ 952 36 93 93

ROSALEDA
A light, spacious centre with more than 100 shops including a bookstore, hairdresser, supermarket, various interior furnishing shops, 14 cinema screens and a video club.
✉ Centro Rosaleda, Avenida Simon Bolivar
☎ 952 88 05 00

MARBELLA

LA CAÑADA COMMERCIAL CENTRE
Shopping centre with individual shops, fast-food restaurants and a supermarket.
✉ Parque Comerical la Cañada, Ctra de Ojén s/n
☎ 952 86 01 42

PUERTO BANÚS

COSTA MARBELLA DEPARTMENT STORE
Gigantic superstore just outside Puerto Banús. Part of the El Corte Inglés chain, with a large hypermarket (Hipercor) on the ground floor and a variety of specialised shops on the upper floors. Underground parking.
✉ Ctra N340, km 174
☎ 952 90 99 90

DEPARTMENT STORES

The mammoth department store has become a sign of the times in Spain and an increasing number are to be found on the Costa del Sol. El Corte Inglés is a household name in Spain. It started trading way back in 1939, selling only English fabric. Over the years the group has expanded into a large chain of stores located all over the country and selling an increasing range of items made in Spain.

Cinema & Theatre

SALON VARIETÉS

Among the various cinemas and theatres along the coast, which can be enjoyed by locals and visitors alike, one place stands out as a rock of entertainment for the English-speaking community. The Salon Varietés, which first opened in Fuengirola in 1985, continues to put on a variety of entertainment each season, from mid-September to mid-June. Audiences can enjoy all types of plays, from thrillers to comedies, musicals and pantomines, concerts, flamenco shows and dance festivals.

CÓRDOBA

GRAN TEATRO

Programme of opera, concerts, ballet and song recitals.
✉ Avenida del Gran Capitán 3
☎ 957 48 02 37; www.teatrocordobo.com

FUENGIROLA

CINE SUR FUENGIROLA MIRAMAR

Original version films shown daily.
✉ Avenida de la Encarnación, Parque Miramar ☎ 952 19 86 00; www.cinesur.som

SALON VARIETÉS

Cinema and theatre for the English-speaking community (▶ panel).
✉ Emancipacón 30
☎ 952 47 45 42

GRANADA

TEATRO ALHAMBRA

Programme of plays in Spanish, as well as ballet, flamenco, classical concerts and jazz.
✉ Molinos 56
☎ 958 22 04 47

MÁLAGA

ALAMEDA MULTICINES

✉ Córdoba 13
☎ 952 21 34 12

ALBEÑIZ MULTICINES

✉ Alcazabilla 4
☎ 952 21 58 98

AMÉRICA MULTICINES

✉ Explanada de la Estación
☎ 952 33 99 91

ANDALUCÍA CINEMA

✉ Victoria 2
☎ 952 21 06 16

TEATRO MIGUEL DE CERVANTES

Spanish-language plays, concerts and flamenco. Concerts by the Málaga Symphony Orchestra in winter.
✉ Ramos Martín s/n
☎ 952 22 41 00; www.teatrocervantes.com

YELMO CINEPLEX

Original version films.
✉ Avenida Alfonso Ponce Léon
☎ 902 20 21 03

PUERTO BANÚS

CINE GRAN MARBELLA

Often films in English.
✉ Puerto Banús ☎ 952 81 00 77; www.cinesgranmarbella.com

MARBELLA

CINE SUR PLAZA DEL MARBELLA

Original version films.
✉ Avenida Camilo José Cela
☎ 952 76 69 42; www.cinesur.com

SEVILLA

TEATRO LOPE DE VEGA

Classical concerts and ballet.
✉ Avenida María Luisa s/n
☎ 954 59 08 67

TEATRO DE LA MAESTRANZA

Sevilla's opera house. Classical music and jazz.
✉ Paseo de Colón s/n
☎ 954 22 33 44; www.teatromaestranza.com

TEATRO MUNICIPAL ALAMEDA

Spanish-language plays, including children's plays.
✉ Calle Crédito 13
☎ 954 38 83 12

Casinos & Discos

CASINOS

BENALMÁDENA COSTA

CASINO TORREQUEBRADA
American and French roulette, Black Jack, Punto Blanco, slot machines and a private gaming room. Formal dress; passport required.
Avenida del Sol 952 44 60 00; www.torrequebrada.com
Daily 8pm–4am Bus stop Benalmádena Costa
Expensive

NUEVA ANDALUCÍA

CASINO MARBELLA
American and French roulette, Black Jack, Stud Caribbean poker, Punto Blanco, slot machines. Jacket and tie for men. Passport required.
Hotel Andalucía Plaza, opposite Puerto Banús, Nueva Andalucía 952 81 40 00; www.casinomarbella.com
Daily 9pm–3am
Bus stop Andalucía Plaza
Expensive

CASINO NUEVO SAN ROQUE
Chic casino offering roulette and Black Jack. Passport, jacket and tie required.
Ctra N340, km 127
965 78 10 00; www.casinosanroque.com

DISCOS

FUENGIROLA

DISOTECA MAXY
A late-night disco for a more mature crowd.
Calle España None

MÁLAGA

LICEO
Attracts local students with its thumping music and fevered atmosphere.
Calle Beatas 21 None

ZZ CLUB
Popular with students with live bands at weekends.
6 Calle Tejón y Rodriguez
None

MARBELLA & PUERTO BANÚS

DREAMERS
Popular venue playing a good variety of music in sumptuous surrounds.
A7, km 175, Puerto Banús
952 81 20 80

LA NOTTE
Seriously glam late-night club for big spenders who like it loud.
17 Casals, Marbella
952 86 69 96

OLIVIA VALERE
Huge dance floor, Moorish-style décor. Passport required.
Ctra de Istán, km 0.8
952 82 88 45

TORREMOLINOS

FUN BEACH
This claims to be the largest disco in Europe with eight dance floors.
Avenida Palma de Mallorca 36 952 38 02 56

PALLADIUM
A popular dancing spot, with trendy lighting and music at full force.
Avenida Palma de Mallorca 36 952 38 42 89

NIGHTLIFE

The Costa is famed for its lively night scene, with an abundance of discos and nightclubs to suit every taste. There is a concentration of discos in Torremolinos, and a wide choice of glitz to be found in and around Marbella, especially Puerto Banús. In Fuengirola and Los Boliches you can find many bars with music, and perhaps karaoke, a number of which are English-run.

Opening times are flexible; however, the action starts late, very late, with minimal activity to be expected before 11pm or midnight. Once things hot up they tend to carry on well into the early hours. Charges are variable, with some discos charging a fairly substantial entrance fee, which usually includes one free drink.

Flamenco & Jazz

JAZZ

Jazz fans have plenty of opportunities to indulge their interest. Numerous cafés and piano bars in the main resorts, in particular Torremolinos, Fuengirola, Marbella and Puerto Banús, offer live music that can include jazz, blues and soul. Concerts are also laid on for visiting musicians. These take place in a variety of venues, such as clubs or some of the more prominent hotels along the coast.

FLAMENCO

Flamenco is closely associated with Andalucía, where its roots belong. For the visitor who wishes to get the flavour of something seen as 'typically Spanish' there are plenty of nightspots along the Costa with flamenco shows, which can be colourful and entertaining. The real magic of flamenco, however, is spontaneity and the right ambience, which is not so easy to find. You could experience some good flamenco at a local fiesta, or tucked away in the back streets of towns such as Sevilla or Málaga, accompanied, ideally, by someone who knows where to look.

BENALMÁDENA COSTA

FORTUNA NIGHTCLUB
International live bands and flamenco.
✉ Casino Torrequebrada, N340 between Benalmádena Costa and Carvaja ☎ 952 44 60 00 🕐 From 9.30pm

CÓRDOBA

MESÓN FLAMENCO LA BULERÍA
✉ Pedro López 3 ☎ 957 48 38 39 🕐 From 10.30pm. Closed Dec–Feb

FUENGIROLA

MOOCHERS JAZZ RESTAURANT
Restaurant with live music in summer. Terrace.
✉ Calle de la Cruz 17 ☎ 952 47 71 54 🕐 Dinner only

GRANADA

JARDINES NEPTUNO
High-quality flamenco.
✉ Calle Arabia ☎ 958 52 25 33 🕐 From 10pm

MÁLAGA

VISTA ANDALUCÍA
This flamenco show has been castanet clicking since 1987 and has a good local reputation.
✉ Avenida Los Guindos 29 ☎ 952 23 11 57 🕐 Tue–Sat at 10.30pm

MANILVA

SEPTIMA CIELO
Bar/restaurant/crêperie, with New Orleans jazz.
✉ Río de Manilva 7 (between Manilva and Estepona) ☎ 952 89 26 90 🕐 Jazz Wed night

MARBELLA

ANA MARIA
Lively bar, with flamenco.
✉ Plaza Santo Cristo 5, Casco Antiquo ☎ 952 77 56 46

LA CASETA DEL CASINO
Flamenco and *sevillanas*.
✉ Casino Nueva Andalucía, Andalucía Plaza Hotel, N340, Nueva Andalucía ☎ 952 81 40 00 🕐 From midnight in summer

NERJA

EL COLONIO
Restaurant with flamenco.
✉ Granada 6 ☎ 952 52 18 26 🕐 Dinner show summer, Wed–Fri 9.30 or 10pm; winter, Wed 9pm

RONDA

CASA SANTA POLA
Attractive restaurant offering flamenco shows and regional dances.
✉ Calle Santo Domingo 3 ☎ 952 87 92 08 🕐 Sat, Sun at 9.30pm

SEVILLA

EL ARENAL
Theatre and restaurant.
✉ Auda M Auxiliadora 18 ☎ 954 53 47 20 🕐 9.30pm, 11.30pm

LOS GALLOS
Small and intimate; top flamenco shows.
✉ Plaza de Santa Cruz ☎ 954 21 69 81 🕐 9, 11.30pm

TORREMOLINOS

TABERNA FLAMENCO PEPE LÓPEZ
Popular for flamenco.
✉ Plaza de la Gamba Alegre ☎ 952 38 12 84 🕐 Apr until autumn at 10pm

Watersports

SAILING

There are excellent facilities for sailing at the major marinas. Most of the marinas and their yacht clubs organise beginners' sailing, monitor and yacht-master classes in summer. Major marinas and yacht clubs include:

La Duqesa	☎ 952 89 01 00
Estepona	☎ 952 80 18 00
Marbella	☎ 952 77 57 00
Fuengirola	☎ 952 46 80 00
Benalmádena	☎ 952 44 30 48
Málaga	☎ 952 22 63 00

SCUBA DIVING

Almuñécar and Nerja, east of Málaga, are good centres for diving. Day courses with qualified instructors are available at:

CENTRO BUCEO TARIFA

A wide range of diving courses, day and night.
✉ Calle Alcalde Juan Nuñez 10 ☎ 956 68 16 48; www.yellowsubtarifa.com

CLUB NAUTICO DIVING CENTRE

Year-round courses, equipment hire included.
✉ Puerto Marina de Benalmádena ☎ 952 56 07 69

FUENGIROLA DIVING CENTRE

Full PADI courses.
✉ Fuengirola port ☎ 952 58 83 12

SWIMMING

Costa del Sol's beaches vary from sand to fine grit and shingle. Some of the best sandy beaches are around Torremolinos, Fuengirola and on either side of Marbella, all of which can become very crowded in the summer season. For more secluded beaches try east of Málaga or west of Estepona.

WATERSKIING AND WIND-AND-KITESURFING

There are plenty of waterskiing and wind-and-kitesurfing opportunities here. Facilities and tuition are available in all major resorts, often from the hotels. The top spot for wind-and-kitesurfing is at Tarifa, where strong winds provide favourable conditions.

LA CABAÑA

Windsurfing only.
✉ Carretera el Lentiscal 1a, Bolonia ☎ 956 68 85 06

CLUB MISTRAL

Windsurfing boards for hire on the beach. Lessons available.
✉ Hotel Hurricane, Tarifa Ctra N340, km 77 ☎ 952 68 49 19; www.club-mistral.com

HOT STICK KITE SURFING

✉ Calle Batalla del Salado 41, Tarifa ☎ 956 68 04 19

SHARKITE KITE SCHOOL TARIFA PILOTS

✉ Calle Batalla del Salado 46 ☎ 956 62 70 05

SURFCENTER DOS MARES

✉ Ctra Cádiz-Málaga, km 79.5, Tarifa ☎ 956 68 40 35

ANDALUCIAN AERIEL SPORTS FEDERATION

☎ 952 60 13 61

CLEAN BEACHES

In the mid-1980s a decree was passed in Andalucía establishing standards of cleanliness on local beaches. The matter is taken very seriously and carefully monitored by the authorities, with the result that an increasing number of beaches proudly display the coveted Blue Flag.

Beaches are classified by 5 to 1 stars according to their condition. Symbols also indicate the 'dos and don'ts', while other signs advertise services available on the beach. Visitors are requested to observe these golden rules: be sure to use a protective sun block, especially where children are concerned; drink plenty of liquid (but do check if the water is safe to drink); make sure any food consumed has been bought in a reputable place; keep the beaches clean by using containers for rubbish disposal; use a mat or towel when relaxing on the sand; do not swim in prohibited areas; respect the 'dangerous to swim' sign; do not take pets onto the beach; camp only in authorised areas that have proper facilities.

Golf

COSTA DEL GOLF

This stretch of coast is often described as the Costa del Golf, as indicated by the occasional signpost along the road. In fact golf has had a tremendous impact on the Costa del Sol, especially during the winter season. The region's mild winter climate, combined with an abundance of high-quality courses, make it a highly desirable year-round golfing destination, sometimes described as the Costa del Golf.

New courses continue to be built to accommodate the ever increasing number of golfers who flock down to the coast. But with courses often filled to capacity, pre-booking is a necessity at certain times.

Spain's hosting of the Ryder Cup in 1997 brought great prestige to the area, earning it international acclaim. It was a matter of great pride to the Costa that Valderrama, in Sotogrande, was the first course selected outside the UK and US to host this great international event.

Since then the region has continued to host numerous international golfing events, attracting top players from all over the world. A number of new courses are in the planning stage.

Green fees for golf courses on the Costa del Sol are among the most competitive in Europe. Many hotels also offer their guests reduced green fees. The following gives an approximate range of current green fees (subject to change and to season):
€ = up to €60
€€ = €60–€90
€€€ = over €90
The majority of golf clubs require a handicap certificate. Courses get booked up by members so reserve well in advance to ensure a game. There are numerous competitions open to visitors throughout the year. Useful publications and organisations include:
Sungolf ✉ Camino Viejo de Coín, Mijas Costa ☎ 952 47 2090; www.sungolf.net
The Federación Andaluza de Golf ✉ Calle Sierra de Grazalema 33, bloque 5, 29016 Málaga ☎ 952 22 55 99/90; www.golf-andalucia.net
Costa de Sol Golf News ✉ Tamisa Hotel, Mijas Costa ☎ 952 58 68 89; www.costadelsolgolfnews.com
Green Life, Cabopino, La Cañada, Flamingos and Baviera are among the golf courses that have opened since 2000. The following are some of the major clubs in the region. Most of the clubs offer classes and instruction.

ALHAURIN GOLF & COUNTRY CLUB (€)
Two 18-hole courses and a 9-hole, par 72.
✉ Ctra Mijas–Alhaurín, Alhaurín el Grand, km 6
☎ 952 59 5800; www.alhauringolf.com

ALOHA GOLF CLUB (€€€)
18 and 9 holes, par 72.
✉ Urb Aloha, Nueva Andalucía
☎ 952 90 70 85; www.clubdegolfaloha.com

LOS ARQUEROS (€€)
18 holes, par 72. This course was Severiano Ballesteros' first design and offers a challenge to golfers of all handicaps.
✉ Finca Torre, Ctra de San Pedro–Ronda, C339, km 5, Benahavis ☎ 952 78 46 00

ATALAYA GOLF AND COUNTRY CLUB (€€€)
18 holes, par 71 and 72
✉ Ctra Benahavis, km 0.7, Estepona ☎ 952 88 28 12; www.atalaya-park.es

LA CALA (€€)
Two 18-hole courses, par 72 and 73.
✉ La Cala de Mijas, Mijas–Costa
☎ 952 66 90 33; www.lacala.com

LA DAME DE NOCHE (€)
9 holes, par 70. A 24-hour course, with floodlighting.
✉ Camino del Angel, Río Verde, Marbella ☎ 952 81 81 50; www.damedenoche.com

LA DUQUESA (€)
18 holes, par 72.
✉ Urb El Hacho, Ctra de Cádiz, N340, km 150, Manilva
☎ 952 89 04 25; www.golfladuquesa.com

EL PARAÍSO (€)
18 holes, par 72.
✉ Ctra de Cádiz, N340, km 167, Estepona ☎ 952 88 38 36; www.elparaisogolfclub.com

ESTEPONA GOLF (€)
18 holes, par 72.
✉ Ctra de Cádiz, N340, km 150

☎ 952 11 30 81; www.esteponagolf.com

GUADALHORCE CLUB DE GOLF (€)
18 and 9 holes, par 72.
✉ Ctra de Cártama, km 7, Campanillas ☎ 952 17 93 68; www.guadalhorce.com

GUADALMINA CLUB DE GOLF (€€)
Two 18-hole courses and a 9-hole, par 72.
✉ Urb Guadalmina Alta, San Pedro de Alcántara ☎ 952 88 33 75; www.guadalminagolf.org

MARBELLA GOLF CLUB (€€)
18 holes, par 72.
✉ Urb El Roasrio, Ctra de Cádiz, N340, km 192, Marbella ☎ 952 83 05 00; www.marbella.net

MIJAS GOLF INTERNATIONAL (€€)
Two courses, par 71 and 72.
✉ Urb Mijas Golf, Mijas Costa ☎ 952 47 68 43; www.mijasgolf.net

MIRAFLORES GOLF (€)
18 holes, par 70. Right up in the hills of Mijas.
✉ Urb Riviera del Sol, Ctra de Cádiz, N340, km 199, Mijas Costa ☎ 952 93 19 60; www.mirafloresgolf.com

MONTEMAYOR GOLF CLUB (€€)
18 holes, par 70.
✉ Avenida Montemayor, Benahavis ☎ 952 93 71 11

LOS NARANJOS (€€)
18 holes, par 72.
✉ Apdo 64, Nueva Andalucía ☎ 952 81 24 28; www.losnaranjos.com

PARADOR DEL GOLF (€)
18 holes, par 72.
✉ About 1 km from Málaga airport ☎ 952 38 12 55

LA QUINTA GOLF & COUNTRY CLUB (€€)
27 holes, par 72. Fine views of the mountains and the Marbella coastline. Training programmes for beginners and more advanced players, also special courses for groups.
✉ Ctra San Pedro–Ronda, C339, km 3 ☎ 952 76 23 90; www.laquintagolf.com

REAL CLUB DE CLUB SOTOGRANDE (€€€)
18 and 9 holes, par 72. Beautiful course designed by Robert Trent.
✉ Paseo del Parque, Sotogrande ☎ 956 78 50 14

SAN ROQUE (€€€)
18 holes, par 72.
✉ Urb San Roque Club, Ctra de Cádiz, N340, km 127, San Roque ☎ 956 61 30 30; www.sanroqueclub.com

SANTA MARIA GOLF & COUNTRY CLUB (€)
18 holes, par 72.
✉ Coto de los Dolores, Urb Elviria. Between Fuengirola and Marbella ☎ 952 83 10 36; www.santamariagolfclub.com

TORREQUEBRADA (€€)
18 and 9 holes, par 72.
✉ Ctra de Cádiz, N340, km 220, Benalmádena Costa ☎ 952 44 27 41; www.golftorrequebrada.com

VALDERRAMA (€€€)
18 holes, par 72.
✉ Ctra de Cádiz, N340, km 132, Sotogrande ☎ 956 79 12 00; www.valderrama.com

SAN ROQUE/SOTOGRANDE

This is *the* place for big-time golfers and is said to feature Spain's highest proportion of registered golfers in any one centre. There are four golf courses. The Valderrama Robert Trent Jones Course played host to the 1997 Ryder Cup and, in April 2005, the Spanish Open Golf Championship was held at San Roque.

The little town of San Roque is an attractive centre in itself with narrow streets and plenty of flowers and plants. The lively cafés and restaurants of the Campamento area appeal to a younger crowd.

POLO

Another string to Sotogrande's bow is the sport of polo, which continues to thrive.

Top-ranking players come here to take part in the numerous matches that are held regularly during the summer months at the Santa María Polo Club. The sport has a substantial following, attracting an enthusiastic crowd. Although a traditional sport, with continuity within families, efforts are being made to popularise it and to bring it to a wider public.

Horseriding & Biking

BENALMÁDENA CABLE CAR

One of the coast's many attractions is the 'Telecabina Benalmádena'. From its starting point, by Tivoli World (Arroyo de la Miel), this 4-person cable car carries you up to the summit of the Calamorro mountain (about 10 minutes). Lookout points offer panoramic views of the whole coast and the Málaga mountains and marked paths offer walks in the area.
Telecabina Benalmádena SA
✉ Explanada Tivoli s/n, Arroyo de la Miel
☎ 952 57 50 38

BULLFIGHTING

Along the Costa del Sol bullfights are held on Sunday afternoons during the summer season in Málaga, Estepona and Marbella. The bigger names, however, are attracted by Sevilla, Córdoba and other prominent towns in Andalucía.

HORSE RACING

The Hipódromo race course in Mijas Costa holds races every Saturday throughout the summer.
✉ Urb El Chaparral, Mijas Costa ☎ 952 59 27 00; www.mijas-races.com

HORSERIDING

ESTEPONA

FINCA SIESTA
Saddle up for picnic and beach rides, or take lessons in dressage and showjumping.
✉ km 163 on N230 (opposite Hacienda Beach)
☎ 952 79 01 89; www.finca-siesta.com

MARBELLA

CLUB HÍPICO ELVIRIA
✉ El Platero, between Marbella and Fuengirola
☎ 952 83 52 72

MARBELLA CLUB HOTEL
An equestrian centre that offers lessons as well as rides.
✉ Boulevard Principe Alfonso de Hohenlohe ☎ 952 82 98 84

LOS MONTEROS RIDING SCHOOL
Lessons and rides while enjoying the picturesque surrounding hills.
✉ Ctra de Cádiz, N340, km 177
☎ 952 77 06 75

NERJA

HORSIN' AROUND
✉ Nerja ☎ 625 89 98 75; www.lake-vinuela.com

SAN PEDRO DE ALCÁNTARA

LAKEVIEW EQUESTRIAN CENTRE
Instruction in dressage and showjumping; lessons can be booked individualy or with a group.
✉ Valle del Sol
☎ 952 78 69 34

SAN ROQUE

THE SAN ROQUE CLUB EQUESTRIAN CENTRE
For beginners and experienced riders. One-hour or full-day trips.
✉ San Roque Club Suites Hotel, Ctra Cádiz, km 126.5
☎ 956 61 30 30; www.sanroqueclub.com

SOTOGRANDE POLO
You can experience the thrill of riding top-class polo ponies on Sotogrande's polo fields.
☎ 956 79 64 64; www.santamariapoloclub.com

TORREMOLINOS

CLUB EL RANCHITO
Full horseriding facilities available.
✉ Camino del Pilar, La Colina
☎ 952 38 31 40

GONZÁLEZ-GARRIDO
✉ J Ctra de Cádiz s/n
☎ 952 38 30 63

For further information about horse riding in rural Andalucía contact:
Asociación de Empresarios de Turismo Equestre de Andalucía (AETEA)
✉ Isla de la Cartuja s/n, 41092 Sevilla ☎ 954 46 00 01

BIKING

Explore the countryside by bicycle or mountain bike.

MONTE AVENTURA
✉ Plaza de Andalucía, Ojén
☎ 952 88 15 19

SIERRA CYCLING
✉ Urb Pueblo Castillo 7, Fuengirola ☎ 925 47 17 20

Tennis & Adventure Activities

TENNIS

Most top hotels along the coast have tennis courts. There are a number of clubs in the area, including:

BENALMÁDENA COSTA

CLUB DE TENIS TORREQUEBRADA
Urb Torrequebrada, Ctra de Cádiz 952 44 60 00

ESTEPONA

CLUB DE TENIS ESTEPONA
10 courts, 3 floodlit; hard and tennis-quick.
Urb Forest Hill
952 80 15 79

FUENGIROLA

AZTEC TENNIS CLUB RIVIERA DEL SOL
Tennis lessons available.
Urb Riviera del Sol, Libra, s/n
952 93 44 77

MARBELLA

CLUB EL CASCO
8 clay courts, 2 floodlit.
Urb El Rosario
952 83 76 51

CENTRO DE TENIS DON CARLOS
11 courts, 4 floodlit; clay and tennis-quick.
Urb Elviria, Ctra de Cádiz
952 83 17 39

CLUB HOTEL LOS MONTEROS
10 courts, 2 floodlit.
Ctra de Cádiz, km 194
952 77 17 00

MANOLO SANTANA RAQUETS CLUB
Ctra de Istán, km 2, Marbella
952 77 85 80;
www.manolosantana.net

CLUB PUENTE ROMANO
5 clay, 4 quick-surface and 2 artificial grass courts.
Hotel Puente Romao, Ctra de Cádiz 952 82 61 03

MIJAS

LEW HOAD CAMPO DE TENIS
Ctra de Mijas
952 47 48 58

SOTOGRANDE

SOTOGRANDE RACQUET CLUB
El Cucurucho Beach Club
956 79 62 33

ADVENTURE ACTIVITIES

The following clubs near Málaga offer hang-gliding and paragliding courses.

CLUB ESCUELA PARAPENTE EL VALLE
Valle de Abdalajís
952 48 91 80

CLUB VUELO LIBRE MÁLAGA
Valle de Abdalajís
952 48 92 98

Explore the hinterland by jeep on a day's mini-safari, over mountainous terrain and through parklands.

AUTOS LARA OF TORREMOLINOS
952 17 14 17

MARBELLA RANGERS JEEP SAFARIS
952 83 30 82

SIERRA NEVADA

The Sierra Nevada is the most southerly ski resort in Europe and one of the highest, which gives it a long season (sometimes lasting well into May). Its proximity to the coast offers the possibility of swimming in the sea and skiing on snowy slopes on the same day! The resort is easily accessible by car from Málaga (161km) and from Granada (35km). There is a daily bus service from Granada.

Sol y Nieve (Sun and Snow)
This ski resort offers good facilities, with ski-lifts and chair-lifts, a tourist complex and all kinds of skiing.
35km from Granada and some 100km from the coast
Dec–Apr

COSTA DEL SOL
practical matters

BEFORE YOU GO

WHAT YOU NEED

● Required
○ Suggested
▲ Not required

Some countries require a passport to remain valid for a minimum period (usually at least six months) beyond the date of entry – contact the embassy or your travel agent for details.

	UK	Germany	USA	Netherlands
Passport (or National Identity Card where applicable)	●	●	●	●
Visa (regulations can change – check before your journey)	▲	▲	▲	▲
Onward or Return Ticket	▲	▲	●	▲
Health Inoculations	▲	▲	▲	▲
Health Documentation (reciprocal agreement document) (➤ 90, Health)	●	●	▲	●
Travel Insurance	○	○	○	○
Driving Licence (national – EU format/national/Spanish translation/international)	●	●	●	●
Car Insurance Certificate (if own car)	●	●	●	●
Car Registration Document (if own car)	●	●	●	●

WHEN TO GO

Average figures for Costa del Sol

High season

Low season

JAN	FEB	MAR	APR	MAY	JUN	JUL	AUG	SEP	OCT	NOV	DEC
16°C	17°C	18°C	21°C	23°C	27°C	29°C	29°C	27°C	23°C	19°C	17°C

Wet   Cloud   Sun   Sunshine & Showers

TIME DIFFERENCES

GMT
12 noon

Spain
1pm

Germany
1pm

USA (NY)
7am

Netherlands
1pm

TOURIST OFFICES

In the UK
Spanish Tourist Office,
22/23 Manchester Square,
London W1M 5AP
☎ (020) 7486 8077
Fax: (020) 7486 8034
www.tourspain.co.uk

In the USA
Tourist Office of Spain,
666 Fifth Avenue 35th,
New York, NY 10103
☎ (212) 265 8822
Fax: (212) 265 8864
www.okspain.org

Tourist Office of Spain,
8383 Wilshire Boulevard,
Suite 960,
Beverley Hills, CA 90211
☎ (323) 658 7188
Fax: (323) 658 1061
www.okspain.org

ARRIVING

Most visitors to the Costa del Sol arrive at Málaga Airport (☎ 952 04 88 38). Spain's national airline, Iberia (☎ 902 40 05 00), operates direct scheduled flights to Málaga from major European and North American cities. The other airport in the region is Sevilla.

Málaga Airport
Kilometres to Málaga city centre

10 kilometres

Journey times	
Train	12 minutes
Bus	20 minutes
Car	20 minutes

Sevilla Airport
Kilometres to Sevilla city centre

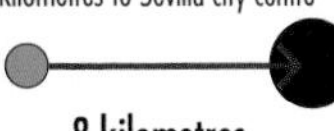

8 kilometres

Journey times	
Train	N/A
Bus	20 minutes
Car	20 minutes

MONEY

The euro (€) is the official currency of Spain. Euro banknotes and coins were introduced in January 2002. Banknotes are issued in denominations of 5, 10, 20, 50, 100, 200 and 500 euros; coins in denominations of 1, 2, 5, 10, 20 and 50 cents, and 1 and 2 euros.
Euro traveller's cheques may be exchanged in banks and exchange offices but the commission may be high and they are not generally accepted for purchases. Credit cards are widely accepted, however, and ATM machines may be used for cash withdrawal, provided you have your PIN number.

TIME

Spain is one hour ahead of Greenwich Mean Time (GMT+1), but from late March until the Saturday before the last Sunday in October, summer time (GMT+2) operates.

CUSTOMS

YES

From another EU country for personal use (guidelines)
800 cigarettes, 200 cigars,
1 kilogram of tobacco
10 litres of spirits (over 22%)
20 litres of aperitifs
90 litres of wine, of which 60 litres can be sparkling wine
110 litres of beer

From a non-EU country for your personal use, the allowances are:
200 cigarettes OR
50 cigars OR
250 grams of tobacco
1 litre of spirits (over 22%)
2 litres of intermediary products (eg sherry) and sparkling wine
2 litres of still wine
50 grams of perfume
0.25 litres of eau de toilette

The value limit for goods is €175
Travellers under 17 years of age are not entitled to the tobacco and alcohol allowances.

NO

Narcotic drugs, firearms, ammunition, offensive weapons, obscene material, unlicensed animals.

CONSULATES

UK
☎ 952 21 75 71
(Málaga)

Germany
☎ 952 21 24 42
(Málaga)

USA
☎ 952 47 48 91
(Fuengirola)

Netherlands
☎ 952 27 99 54
(Málaga)

TOURIST OFFICES

Costa del Sol

- Costa del Sol Tourist Board
  ☎ 952 05 86 94/95;
  www.visitcostadelsol.com

Towns/Resorts

- Plaza San Sebastián 7, Antequera
  ☎ 952 70 25 05;
  www.turismoantequera.com
- Avenida Antonio Machado 10, Benalmádena Costa
  ☎ 952 44 24 94
- Avenida San Lorenzo 1, Estepona
  ☎ 952 80 09 13;
  www.infoestepona.com
- Avenida Jesús Santos Rein 6, Fuengirola
  ☎ 952 46 74 57;
  www.fuengirola.org
- Pasaje de Chinitas 4, Málaga
  ☎ 952 21 34 45;
  www.ayto.malaga.es
- Glorieta de la Fontanilla, Marbella
  ☎ 952 77 14 42;
  www.marbella.es
- Calle Puerta del Mar 4, Nerja
  ☎ 952 52 15 31; www.nerja.org
- Avenida Marqués del Duero 69, San Pedro de Alcántara
  ☎ 952 7852 52
- Avenida de Andalucía 119, Torre del Mar
  ☎ 952 54 11 04
- Ayuntamiento, Plaza Pablo Picasso, Torremolinos
  ☎ 952 37 95 12;
  www.ayto-torremolinos.org

NATIONAL HOLIDAYS

J	F	M	A	M	J	J	A	S	O	N	D
2	1	(3)	(3)	1	1	1	1		1	1	3

1 Jan	New Year's Day
6 Jan	Epiphany
28 Feb	Andalusian Day (regional)
Mar/Apr	Maundy Thursday, Good Friday, Easter Monday
1 May	Labour Day
24 Jun	San Juan (regional)
25 Jul	Santiago (regional)
15 Aug	Assumption of the Virgin
12 Oct	National Day
1 Nov	All Saints' Day
6 Dec	Constitution Day
8 Dec	Feast of the Immaculate Conception
25 Dec	Christmas Day

OPENING HOURS

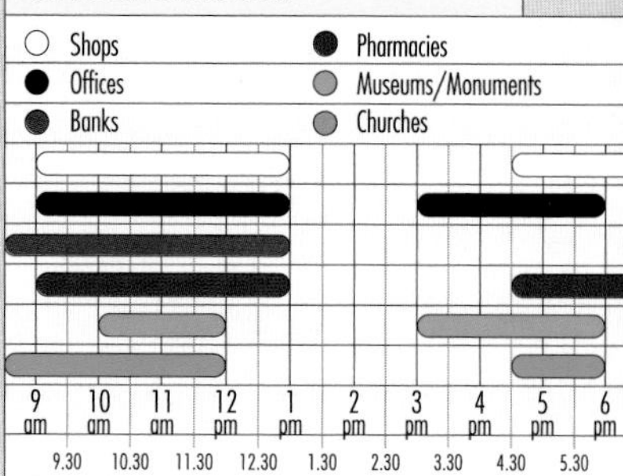

In addition to the times shown above, department stores, large supermarkets and shops in tourist resorts open from 10am through to 8, 9 or even 10pm. Most shops close Sunday and some in August. Some banks open Saturday 9–2 (October–May only). The opening times of museums can vary: some open longer in summer, while hours may be reduced in winter. Many museums close Sunday afternoon, some also on Saturday afternoon, as well as Monday or another day in the week. Some museums offer free entry to EU citizens (take your passport).
Remember – all opening times are subject to change.

ELECTRICITY

The power supply is: 220/230 volts (in some bathrooms and older buildings: 110/120 volts).

Type of socket: two-hole sockets taking round plugs of two round pins. British visitors will need an adaptor and US visitors a voltage transformer.

TIPS/GRATUITIES

Yes ✓ No ✗

Restaurants (if service not included)	✓	5–8%
Cafés/bars	✓	change
Tour guides	✓	change
Hairdressers	✓	change
Taxis	✓	2–3%
Chambermaids	✓	change
Porters	✓	change
Theatre/cinema usherettes	✓	change
Cloakroom attendants	✓	change
Toilets	✓	change

PUBLIC TRANSPORT

Internal Flights The national airline, Iberia, plus the smaller Spanair, operate an extensive network of internal flights. Check the websites www.iberia.com and www.spanair.com. Alternatively, both airlines have offices at the airport. National flights are not cheap but worth considering if you are in a hurry.

Trains Services are provided by the state-run company – RENFE. Fares are among the cheapest in Europe. A useful service is the coastal route from Málaga to Fuengirola, via Torremolinas and Benalmádena, with a stop at the airport.
Trains run every 30 minutes between 7am and 11pm (RENFE ☎ 902 24 02 02; www.renfe.es).

Buses There is a comprehensive and reliable bus network operated by different companies along the coast and to inland towns and villages. Fares are very reasonable. Go to the local bus station for details of routes. The bus station in Málaga (☎ 952 35 00 61) is just behind the RENFE train station.

Ferries A service runs from Málaga to Melilla (Morocco), run by Trasmediterránea Málaga (☎ 902 45 46 45; www.trasmediterranea.es), taking 10 hours. A shorter route to Morocco is from Algeciras to Ceuta (1.5 hours) and Tangier – via Gibraltar – (2.5 hours) run by Trasmediterránea (☎ 956 66 52 00), and Transtour (☎ 956 65 37 06).

Urban Transport Traffic in the main towns and resorts of the Costa del Sol is normally heavy, especially in summer, but public transport in the form of buses is generally good. From the RENFE station there is a bus which runs every 10 minutes or so to the city centre.

CAR HIRE

The leading international car hire companies operate on the Costa del Sol and you can hire a car in advance (essential at peak periods) either direct or through a travel agent. Airlines may offer 'fly-drive' deals. Hiring from a local firm, though, is usually cheaper.

TAXIS

Only use taxis which display a licence issued by the local authority. Taxis show a green light when available for hire. They can be flagged down in the street. In cities and large towns taxis are metered. Where they are not, determine the price of the journey in advance.

CONCESSIONS

Students/Youths Holders of an International Student Identity Card (ISIC) or Euro 26 card may be able to obtain some concessions on travel, entrance fees etc, but the Costa del Sol is not really geared up for students (special facilities and programmes are limited). The main advantage for students and young people is that low-cost package deals are available.

Senior Citizens The Costa del Sol is an excellent destination for older travellers – travel agents offer tailored package holidays. In the winter months there are special low-cost, long-stay holidays for senior citizens. The best deals are available through tour operators who specialise in holidays for senior citizens.

DRIVING

Speed limits on *autopistas* (toll motorways) and *autovías* (free motorways): **120kph**; dual carriageways and roads with overtaking lanes: **100kph**. Take care on the N340 coastal highway. Cars travel at tremendous speed and this road is labelled as a dangerous one.

Speed limits on country roads: **90kph**

Speed limits on urban roads: **50kph**; in residential areas: **20kph**

Seatbelts must be worn in front seats at all times and in rear seats where fitted.

…om breath-testing. Never drive under the influence of alcohol.

Lead-free petrol (*gasolina sin plomo*) is readily available (95 and 98 octane), as is diesel (*gasoleo* or *gasoil*). Petrol stations open 6am–10pm, Mon–Sat. Larger ones open 24 hours. Most take credit cards. There are few petrol stations in the remote inland areas and they may not carry a full range of fuels.

If you break down with your own car and are a member of a motoring organization with a reciprocal agreement (such as AA or RAC in the UK) you can contact the Real Automóvil Club de España (RACE) ☎ 902 40 45 45, which has English-speaking staff and offers 24-hour breakdown assistance. Most international rental firms provide a rescue service.

PHOTOGRAPHY

What to photograph: the rugged coast, unspoilt inland villages, examples of Moorish architecture and panoramas of the Sierra Nevada.
Best times to photograph: the summer sun can be too bright at the height of the day, making photos taken at this time appear 'flat'. It is best to take photographs in the early morning or late evening.
Where to buy film: film (*rollo/carrete*) and camera batteries (*pilas*) are readily available from tourist shops, department stores and photo shops.

PERSONAL SAFETY

The main crimes against visitors are handbag- and camera-snatching, pick-pocketing, theft of unattended baggage and car break-ins. Any crime should be reported to the Policía Nacional.

- Do not leave valuables on the beach or poolside.
- Place valuables in a hotel safety-deposit box.
- Wear handbags and cameras across your chest.
- Avoid lonely, seedy and dark areas at night.

Emergency Telephone Number:
☎ 112
from any call box

TELEPHONES

All telephone numbers in Spain now consist of nine digits. A public telephone (*teléfono*) takes coins or phonecards (*tarjetas telefónicas*), which are sold at post offices and *tabacos* for €6 and €12.
To call Spain from the UK dial 00 34.

International Dialling Codes	
From Spain to:	
UK:	00 44
Germany:	00 49
USA:	00 1
Netherlands:	00 31

Internet cafés are common throughout the Costa del Sol resorts; the respective local tourist office can provide you with a list.

POST

Post Offices

Post offices (*correos*) are generally open as below. In main centres they may open extended hours. Málaga's main post office is at Avenida de Andalucía 1.
Mon–Sat 9–2 (1pm Sat)
☎ 902 29 72 97
Stamps (*sellos*) can also be bought at tobacconists.

HEALTH

Insurance
The European Health Insurance Card (EHIC) replaces the former E111 certificate. This entitles all UK residents to reduced cost (sometimes free) health care. To get an EHIC apply online at dh.gov.uk/travellers or pick up an application from your local Post Office. Non EU citizens must carry private health insurance.

Dental Services
Dental treatment normally has to be paid for in full as dentists operate privately. A list of *dentistas* can be found in the yellow pages of the telephone directory. Dental treatment should be covered by private medical insurance.

Sun Advice
The sunniest (and hottest) months are July and August, when daytime temperatures are often into the 30s (°C). Try to avoid the midday sun and always use a high-factor sun block. Allow yourself to become used to the sun gradually.

Medication
Prescriptions and non-prescription drugs and medicines are available from pharmacies (*farmácias*), distinguished by a large green cross. They are able to dispense many drugs that would be available only on prescription in other countries.

Safe Water
Tap water is chlorinated and generally safe to drink. However, unfamiliar water may cause mild abdominal upsets. Mineral water (*agua mineral*) is cheap and widely available. It is sold *sin gas* (still) and *con gas* (carbonated).

LANGUAGE

Spanish is one of the easiest languages. All vowels are pure and short (as in English). Some useful tips on speaking: 'c' is lisped before 'e' and 'i', otherwise hard; 'h' is silent; 'j' is pronounced like a gutteral 'j'; 'r' is rolled; 'v' sounds more like 'b'; and 'z' is the same as a soft 'c'. English is widely spoken in the principal resorts but you will get a better reception if you at least try communicating with Spaniards in their own tongue.
More extensive coverage can be found in the AA's *Essential Spanish Phrase Book,* which lists over 2,000 phrases and 2,000 words.

hotel	*hotel*	breakfast	*desayuno*
room	*habitación*	toilet	*lavabo*
single/double	*individual/doble*	bath	*baño*
one/two nights	*una/dos noche(s)*	shower	*ducha*
per person	*por persona*	en suite	*en su habitación*
room	*habitación*	balcony	*balcón*
reservation	*reserva*	key	*llave*
rate	*precio*	chambermaid	*camarera*

bank	*banco*	bank card	*tarjeta del banco*
exchange office	*oficina de cambio*	credit card	*tarjeta de crédito*
post office	*correos*	giro bank card	*tarjeta de la caja postal*
cashier	*cajero*		
money	*dinero*	cheque	*cheque*
coin	*moneda*	traveller's cheque	*cheque de viajero*
foreign currency	*moneda extranjera*	giro cheque	*cheque postal*
change money	*cambiar dinero*		
pound sterling	*libra esterlina*		
American dollar	*dólar estadounidense*		

restaurant	*restaurante*	snack	*merienda*
bar	*bar*	starter	*primer plato*
table	*mesa*	dish	*plato*
menu	*carta*	main course	*plato principal*
tourist menu	*menú turístico*	dessert	*postre*
wine list	*carta de vinos*	drink	*bebida*
lunch	*almuerzo*	waiter	*camarero*
dinner	*cena*	bill	*cuenta*

aeroplane	*avión*	ferry	*transbordador*
airport	*aeropuerto*	port	*puerto*
train	*tren*	ticket	*billete*
... station	*estación de ferrocarril*	... single/return	*ida/ida y vuelta*
bus	*autobús*	... first-/second-class	*primera/segunda clase*
... station	*estación de autobUses*	timetable	*horario*
		seat	*asiento*
... stop	*parada de autobús*	non-smoking	*no fumador*

yes	*sí*	help!	*ayuda!*
no	*no*	today	*hoy*
please	*por favor*	tomorrow	*mañana*
thank you	*gracias*	yesterday	*ayer*
hello	*hola*	how much?	*¿cuánto?*
goodbye	*adiós*	expensive	*caro*
good night	*buenas noches*	open	*abierto*
excuse me	*perdóneme*	closed	*cerrado*

WHEN DEPARTING

REMEMBER

- Remember to contact the airport or airline on the day prior to leaving to ensure that the flight details are unchanged.
- There is no airport departure tax to pay.

Index

TwinPack
Costa del Sol

Written by Mona King **Updated by** Jo Hodgson
Revision management by Apostrophe S Limited
Designed and produced by AA Publishing
Series editor Cathy Hatley

A CIP catalogue record for this book is available from the British Library.

ISBN 978-0-7495-4336-5

Published by AA Publishing, a trading name of Automobile Association Developments Limited, whose registered office is Fanum House, Basing View, Basingstoke, Hampshire, RG21 4EA. Registered number 1878835.

First published 2003. Revised second edition 2005.
Reprinted 2005.
Reprinted 2007. Information verified and upated.

Colour separation by Keenes, Andover
Printed and bound by Times Publishing Limited, Malaysia

ACKNOWLEDGEMENTS
The Automobile Association wishes to thank the following libraries and photographers for their assistance with the preparation of this book:
ANDALUCIA SLIDE LIBRARY/MICHELLE CHAPLOW front cover (e) sunbather, 29t, 29b; CORBIS UK/JIM ZUCKERMAN 40b.
The remaining photographs are held in the Association's own photo library (AA World Travel Library, 01256 491588) and were taken by the following photographers:
PETER BAKER 90br; MICHELLE CHAPLOW front cover (a) Torre de la Calahorra, (g) pottery, (h) hibiscus, bottom flowers, Back cover ct (pottery), 6/7, 18t, 21t, 21b, 23, 27t, 27b, 28b, 31b, 33b, 41t, 41b, 49t, 61t, 84; JERRY EDMANSON 15b, 16, 28t, 31t, 32b, 38t, 57; MAX JOURDAN front cover (c) umbrella; ANDREW MOLYNEUX front cover (f) flamenco dancer, Back cover b (Giralda tower), 46t, 85b; KEN PATERSON 85t; JENS POULSEN 13b, 20, 25b, 36, 37b, 40t, 49b; DOUGLAS ROBERTSON Back cover cb (restaurant), 17, 32t, 33t, 43b, 45t, 50; JAMES TIMS front cover (b) bullfighter, (d) Cordoba, Great Mosque, 1, 5t, 5b, 12c, 13t, 14, 18b, 24t, 24b, 25t, 26t, 26b, 30t, 30b, 34t, 37t, 38b, 39t, 39b, 42t, 42b, 51t, 51b, 52t, 52b, 53, 56t, 56b, 90t, 90bl; WYN VOYSEY 15t; PETER WILSON Back cover t (Alcazaba), 12t, 12b, 19t, 19b, 34b, 35t, 35b, 43t, 44t, 44b, 45b, 46b, 47t, 47b, 48t, 48b, 55, 60, 61b.
AA WORLD TRAVEL LIBRARY HISTORICAL COLLECTION 9

A02696
Fold out map © Freytag-Berndt u. Artaria KG, 1231 Vienna-Austria, all rights reserved
Cover maps © ISTITUTO GEOGRAFICO DE AGOSTINI, Novara

TITLES IN THE TWINPACK SERIES
• Algarve • Corfu • Costa Blanca • Costa del Sol • Cyprus • Gran Canaria •
• Lanzarote & Fuerteventura • Madeira • Mallorca • Malta & Gozo • Menorca • Tenerife •
PUBLISHED IN SPRING 2007
• Crete • Croatia

Dear **TwinPack** Traveller

Your comments, opinions and recommendations are very important to us. So please help us to improve our travel guides by taking a few minutes to complete this simple questionnaire.

You do not need a stamp (unless posted outside the UK). If you do not want to cut this page from your guide, then photocopy it or write your answers on a plain sheet of paper.

Send to: **The Editor, AA TwinPack Travel Guides, FREEPOST SCE 4598, Basingstoke RG21 4GY.**

Your recommendations...

We always encourage readers' recommendations for restaurants, nightlife or shopping – if your recommendation is used in the next edition of the guide, we will send you a ***FREE* AA TwinPack Guide** of your choice. Please state below the establishment name, location and your reasons for recommending it.

____

____

____

____

Please send me **AA TwinPack**

Algarve ☐ Corfu ☐ Costa Blanca ☐ Costa del Sol ☐ Crete ☐
Croatia ☐ Cyprus ☐ Gran Canaria ☐ Lanzarote & Fuerteventura ☐
Madeira ☐ Mallorca ☐ Malta & Gozo ☐ Menorca ☐ Tenerife ☐
(*please tick as appropriate*)

About this guide...

Which title did you buy?

AA *TwinPack* ______________________________

Where did you buy it? ______________________________

When? m m / y y

Why did you choose an AA *TwinPack* Guide? ____________________

____

____

____

____

Did this guide meet your expectations?

Exceeded ☐ Met all ☐ Met most ☐ Fell below ☐

Please give your reasons ______________________________

____

____

continued on next page...

Were there any aspects of this guide that you particularly liked? ______________________

____

____

Is there anything we could have done better? ______________________

____

____

About you...

Name (*Mr/Mrs/Ms*) ____

Address ____

____

______________________ Postcode ______________________

Daytime tel no ____

Please only give us your mobile phone number if you wish to hear from us about other products and services from the AA and partners by text or mms.

Which age group are you in?

Under 25 ❑ 25–34 ❑ 35–44 ❑ 45–54 ❑ 55–64 ❑ 65+ ❑

How many trips do you make a year?

Less than one ❑ One ❑ Two ❑ Three or more ❑

Are you an AA member? Yes ❑ No ❑

About your trip...

When did you book? m m / y y When did you travel? m m / y y

How long did you stay? ____

Was it for business or leisure? ____

Did you buy any other travel guides for your trip?

If yes, which ones? ____

Thank you for taking the time to complete this questionnaire. Please send it to us as soon as possible, and remember, you do not need a stamp (*unless posted outside the UK*).

Happy Holidays!

The information we hold about you will be used to provide the products and services requested and for identification, account administration, analysis, and fraud/loss prevention purposes. More details about how that information is used is in our privacy statement, which you'll find under the heading "Personal Information" in our terms and conditions and on our website: www.theAA.com. Copies are also available from us by post, by contacting the Data Protection Manager at AA, Fanum House, Basing View, Basingstoke, Hampshire RG21 4EA.

We may want to contact you about other products and services provided by us, or our partners (by mail, telephone) but please tick the box if you DO NOT wish to hear about such products and services from us by mail or telephone. ❑